# HISTORIC DISASTERS OF RICHMOND

WALTER S. GRIGGS JR.

*To Anne Beale with best wishes [signature] 2016*

THE
History
PRESS

Published by The History Press
Charleston, SC
www.historypress.net

First published 2016

Manufactured in the United States

ISBN 978.1. 46711.886.6

Library of Congress Control Number: 2015956826

*This book is dedicated to my wife, Frances Pitchford Griggs, and to my daughter, Cara Frances Griggs.*

*This book is also dedicated to the Henrico County Division of Fire, to Henrico Doctor's Hospital, to the clergy and members of Second Presbyterian Church and to the many friends and students who expressed their concern for me when I needed it most.*

# CONTENTS

# PREFACE

Disasters have been a part of the human experience since the dawn of history. Some are caused by nature, some by war, some by carelessness, some by disease and some by something as small as a virus. In earlier centuries, there were no ways to stop disasters. Today, we have ways to extinguish fires and fight disease, but we are still helpless when there are floods, hurricanes and storms. Hopefully in the future, there will be better ways to control events before they become full-blown disasters.

This book covers a number of the disasters that have engulfed Richmond and the surrounding area. I have tried to include a variety of different types of disasters: some catastrophic and some that had an impact on only a small group of people. But in all cases, the disaster challenged the human spirit and the will to survive.

# ACKNOWLEDGEMENTS

I want to thank my wife, Frances Pitchford Griggs, for proofreading and editing the manuscript and my daughter, Cara F. Griggs, for helping me with the pictures and research. I also want to acknowledge the support of the archives reference staff of the Library of Virginia, Chesterfield County; Henrico County Division of Fire; and the Pickett Society.

Once again, I want to thank J. Banks Smither, Katie Stitely and Katie Parry of The History Press for their support and encouragement. Also, I want to acknowledge the support of Bob and Sue Griggs, Marianne Miller, Elliott "Chip" Minor, Glenn Gilbreath, Jerry Becker, Susan Robbins, Bob Wood, Pat and Dick Harwood, Carolyn Whitworth Brittain, Ann Williams and Anne P. Bryant.

## Introduction

# A NIGHT TO FORGET

It seemed like a simple assignment for Virginia Commonwealth University, where I served as a department chairman. I was to fly to Boston, Massachusetts; check into the Sheraton Boston Hotel; attend an academic meeting; and recruit faculty members to teach statistics. I boarded the Eastern Airline plane at Byrd Airport, flew to Boston, checked into the hotel, went to my room on the twelfth floor of the twenty-nine-floor hotel and then went to a large room and started looking for faculty prospects.

After a long day of futile recruiting, I returned to my room, number 1229, and began reading a book about the history of the world by Hendrik Willem van Loon. I read this paragraph, which fascinated me:

> *High up in the North in the land called Svithjod, there stands a rock. It is a hundred miles high and a hundred miles wide. Once every thousand years a little bird comes to this rock to sharpen its beak. When the rock has thus been worn away, then a single day of eternity will have gone by.*

I must have fallen asleep thinking about that little bird, but around 2:30 a.m., I was awakened by the sirens of fire engines that seemed to be coming from all over the place and circling the hotel. But for some reason, I did not think they were coming to the Sheraton Boston Hotel. I was trying to go back to sleep when someone began pounding on the door. I thought it was some sort of party going on until I opened the door and looked into the soot-covered face of a Boston firefighter. He did not look like a partygoer! He told me to follow him down the fire escape through the choking smoke that was filling the building. The smoke was so thick I could hardly see the firefighter who was leading me to safety, but I followed his flashlight as smoke filled the stairwell. After finally getting to the first floor, I went to a large room and tried to stop coughing. In the room, people were praying, telling jokes or just resting. The room was being used for a display of medical equipment. A large group of people were huddled in a corner, being led in prayer by a priest. Later, I learned that one guest was saved by a mouse that was running around his trash can and making a noise. The noise woke him up; the fate of the heroic mouse is unknown. A Red Cross volunteer asked me and an American Airlines captain to give out bedroom slippers. Finally, I felt that I was doing something useful.

To get some fresh air, I went outside and called my wife at 3:30 a.m. from a pay phone. I did not want her to hear about the fire on the radio. (I did not realize that she would not be listening to the radio or television in the middle of the night.) Soon, I learned that the nearby Copley Plaza Hotel was also on fire. I walked the streets of Boston, watched the firefighters carry people out of the hotel and took pictures of the fire engines with the camera I managed to grab from my room as I was leaving. There were

A Boston fire engine at the Sheraton Boston Hotel fire. *Photograph by Walter S. Griggs Jr.*

plenty of opportunities to take pictures since every fire engine in Boston, along with units from adjoining jurisdictions, had responded to the two fires. Then I got angry when I learned that a disgruntled employee had set the hotels on fire. Someone I did not know had tried to kill me and everyone else in the hotel.

The two blazes caused 1,800 guests to leave their rooms, sent 64 people to the hospital and resulted in several deaths. One man said, "Thank God for the Boston Fire Department." I could only respond, "Amen!"

The next morning, I was able to retrieve my suitcase, which smelled of smoke. If you had your hotel key, you were treated to a free breakfast provided by the hotel. I had my key. Later in the day, I returned home on a Piedmont flight. I was very happy to see my family again. I had survived the fire, but I did not find a statistics professor.

Although this happened in 1979, I still sometimes jump when someone knocks on my office door. My mind races back to that night in a hotel filling with smoke, a fireman pounding on my door and how I narrowly avoided choking to death. Even today, I keep a picture of a Boston fire engine in my office to remind me of the night disaster struck in Boston.

Disasters like the Boston fire make the news. People still remember explosions, hurricanes, tornadoes, epidemics and fires. These events make interesting stories that add to the human experience. And Richmond, Virginia, has had its share of disasters, both natural and man-made.

## Chapter 1

# TWO FLOODS TWO HUNDRED YEARS APART

## 1771 AND 1972

Since the biblical story of Noah, floods have been viewed as destructive to humankind. The story of the ark is widely known—Noah knew a flood was coming and was able to prepare for it. Can you imagine a world where there were no weather forecasts, and you would never know what to expect, weather wise, from day to day? You could not turn on your computer, TV or radio and get an updated weather forecast. To be safe, you would have to carry a raincoat and umbrella every day, since you would never know what to expect from the weather. But this was the case in the 1700s. Farmers never knew when rain would wipe out their crops or a drought would cause corn to wither away in the fields. Sailors used to cross the Atlantic without knowing what to expect, and the large number of shipwrecks are a testimony to their being caught in a hurricane or violent storm without warning.

By most accounts, the worst flood in Richmond's history came as a surprise on May 27, 1771. It was not raining in Richmond when the flood surged down the James River and inundated the River City. Unbeknownst to most Richmonders, it had been raining for ten or twelve days in the mountains, and the water was flooding the rivers. Soon, Richmonders saw that the James River had risen above all previous flood levels and was overflowing its banks, but they could do nothing about it except wonder how long the flood would last as the water rose to a height of forty feet above flood stage. This flood has been described as "a wall of water roaring down the James River Valley." It swept through Richmond, destroyed buildings and boats and killed about 150 people.

The *Virginia Gazette* of May 30, 1771, published in Williamsburg, Virginia, carried the following account of the flood:

> *There is now the greatest Freshet* [flood] *in James River ever known, it being at least twenty Feet higher than that in May 1766. The Warehouses at Westham are entirely gone, with three Hundred Hogsheads of Tobacco. At Byrd's Warehouse, the Water is now Half Way up the Lower Tier of Hogsheads; the other Warehouse of Shockoe are almost under Water, and the Tobacco drifting away by thirty and forty Hogsheads at a Time. It is imagined there might have been about three Thousand Hogshead in the different Warehouses at Shockoe. Almost every lumber house is gone, and destroyed, on each Side of the River…The Ships in the River were in most imminent Danger, from the vast Number of huge Trees driving down, the Rapidity of the Current and many of them have sustained great Damage. The Ships at Shirley Hundred were driven from their mooring over to City Point and those at City Point down as low as Jordan's.*

Contemporary letters tell a graphic story. John Howard of Botetourt County wrote the following letter on June 6, 1771:

> *I understand all of my Crop of Tobacco that was growing is ruined as well as all that was in the Tobacco House about 6 Hogsheads together with all my Tobacco Houses except one, are swept away, and 13 Hogsheads, sent to the Warehouse, or Westham, I suppose are gone, as I hear the water was over both places, my Corn House with the Corn swept away & some of my stock, and it is owing to the great goodness of God that my People are all alive.*

The *Virginia Gazette* of June 6, 1771, published another article, which gave more detail:

> *From Richmond we learn that they receive daily Accounts of the Devolution occasioned by the late flood. From the Mountains to the Falls, the low grounds have been swept of almost every Thing valuable, and the land is so much ruined that it is thought not to be of Half its former Value, and a great Part is entirely ruined. Fourteen Negroes belonging to one estate were drowned…Between six and seven Hundred Head of Cattle, Hogs, and Sheep have been lost, and near a hundred horses…There were no Rains to speak of at Richmond so that they must have fallen from the Mountains.*

On August 1, 1771, Richard Bland wrote the following letter to Thomas Adams:

*Upon the 27ᵗʰ of May, a most dreadful Inundation happened in James, Rappahannock and Roanoke Rivers occasioned by very heavy and incessant Rains upon the mountains for ten or twelve days…Promiscuous Heaps of Houses, Trees, Men, Horses, Cattle, Sheep, Hogs, Merchandise, Corn, Tobacco & every other thing that was unfortunately within the dreadful sweep were seen Floating upon the Waters, without a possibility of their being saved.*

The flood was devastating, and it prompted the assembly to issue thirty thousand pounds in treasury notes for the tobacco lost at public warehouses. With the passage of time, this flood has been largely forgotten. The passing years have erased all of the damage caused by the greatest flood in Richmond's history.

Although not often noticed, there is a monument that mentions the flood on Turkey Island in Henrico County with the following inscription:

*Foundation of this pillar was laid in the calamitous year 1771 when all the great rivers of this country were swept by inundations never before experienced which changed the face of nature and left traces of their violence that will remain for ages.*

A monument on Turkey Island in memory of the Randolph family; it also commemorates the great flood of 1771. *Photograph courtesy of the Pickett Society.*

Henrico County has also placed a marker at the site on Route 5, west of the intersection with Willis Church Road.

Richmonders who lived through the flood that preceded the American Revolution certainly remembered the day "when the great rivers of this country were swept by inundations never before experienced." A little over two hundred years later, a second major flood hit Richmond, but it did not surprise anyone. It was predicted. It was called Agnes.

On June 18, 1972, the *Richmond Times-Dispatch* reported the naming of the first hurricane of the season. The name assigned was Agnes. The Associated Press set the tone for a series of errors when it called the hurricane Agnew, the name of the vice president of the United States, instead of Agnes. But it is doubtful many Richmonders paid much attention to the story even though winds were reaching ninety-five miles per hour as Agnes left the Yucatan Channel at the western tip of Cuba. By June 19, merchants in some Florida communities had been told to evacuate as Hurricane Agnes drew near. Like most hurricanes, Agnes was projected to hit Florida and then pass into history. But Agnes was not like most hurricanes. Instead of passing into history, Agnes was destined to make history. Roaring through the South, Agnes merged with another storm over the Virginia Capes and turned toward Virginia. In summary, Agnes started out as a moderate hurricane and ended up as a tropical storm. With the storm getting closer, Richmonders began to pay attention.

When I heard Agnes was headed toward Virginia, I left early for a professional meeting in the Midwest. Suffice it to say, it was one of my better decisions. I missed all of the excitement—if living through a flood can be termed excitement.

The *Richmond Times-Dispatch* reported on June 21 that Richmond was dark and wet. The reporter wrote, "The waters of tropical storm Agnes were closing in from the north and west but had not yet reached the metropolitan areas and the 'menace still was more shadow that substance.'" But the day was not without its grim omens. By late afternoon, eighty trees had blown over. Agnes had announced its arrival.

The next day, Richmonders were told that the recently completed flood control plan had been implemented. The plan included placing six thousand sandbags at points along the James River and closing the dikes to protect the lower parts of the city. Residents in the threatened area were advised to take the necessary steps to protect their property "from possible exposure to flood water from the James River." The words from the book of Genesis were appropriate: "And the waters prevailed and were increased greatly upon the earth."

The James River was rising from the waters Agnes had dumped into the mountain streams that roared into the James River. As the flood worsened, Interstate Highway 95 was closed out of concern that a dam might give way and flood the highway. The James River was beginning to leave its banks. The business area was becoming increasingly vacant and dark as people tried to get home before power was lost. The newspaper reported: "Downtown offices were plunged into darkness; elevators stopped wherever they happened to be trapping some people between floors and a radio station went off the air." But this power outage was only a precursor of more problems that were to be delivered by Agnes.

Parker Field, now known as the Diamond, was the site of the City of Richmond's command post, the place where the local government had relocated from city hall. Also, the Red Cross and the Salvation Army set up evacuation centers in several locations in the East End of Richmond in preparation for the oncoming flood. All that could be done had been done; now Richmonders could only wait. As the waters surged down the James, three of the bridges across the James were closed: the Boulevard Bridge; the Fourteenth Street Bridge; and the Ninth Street Bridge. The Lee Bridge carried the bulk of the traffic, but traffic jams soon developed. It was now difficult to cross the James because of the lack of open bridges and because people crossing the bridge drove slowly to see the James River go mad.

Meanwhile, sandbags were placed along Dock and Cary Streets. It was a futile effort. The Shockoe Valley pumping station at Seventeenth and Byrd Streets was put out of commission; thus, nothing stood in the way of the James from pushing floodwaters through the sewer system. A reporter wrote, "It was a gray, drizzly day and the contrast of National Guardsmen who had been activated and deserted streets and closed stores prompted one man to think of an 'occupied city.'" The floodwaters soon flowed into lower Main Street and on to Broad at Seventeenth Street. The James also overflowed its banks on the south side of the city, flooding buildings and roads.

Then, Agnes ensured itself a place in history when Richmond's sixty-six-million-gallon-per-day water purification plant was flooded. It was not long before turning on a faucet was a futile effort. Governor Linwood Holton urged everyone to conserve water. Shaving, bathing, diaper washing and a host of ordinary activities were no longer possible. Since Richmond is a genteel city, there was no mention that people might start to stink nor were there any published accounts of any raids on deodorant.

Downtown Richmond was now cordoned off because of flooding, power failures, the closing of bridges and many other reasons. Barricades were erected and manned by the police and National Guard. To supply drinking water, the army brought in tanks of water from as far away as Ohio, and local communities that still had water shared it with Richmond. The tankers were stationed throughout the city. Richmonders lined up at these tankers carrying every type of container to fill with water. Within a couple of days, the filtration plant was restored, and water went back into the lines, but not for drinking—it was good only for flushing toilets and fighting fires.

On June 23, the *Richmond Times-Dispatch* ran an editorial as follows: "Rain ending a long devastating drought can be one of the most welcomed sights in the human experience. But when the water pours from the sky in excessive quantities over a short period of time, the rain itself can be vastly destructive, as Virginia is witnessing so graphically today."

On June 24, the floodwaters reached up to Seventeenth and Broad Streets, entered the second floors of Shockoe Valley businesses and crawled up the steps of Richmond's Main Street Station. The water also inundated Fulton and, on the south side, went up to Commerce Road. Only the Lee Bridge was open to traffic, and traffic was backed up seven miles. As a result of this flood and similar events that have closed the bridges, some native Richmonders still refuse to live south of the James for fear of bridge closings. In addition to the closing of bridges, Amtrak stopped running its trains through Virginia, all weather gages along the James River were knocked out and about fifty new highway department trucks were flooded.

On June 27, the *Richmond Times-Dispatch* published a list of places where water could be obtained. Places included: Hotchkiss Field, the Mosque Parking Lot, Pollard Park at Brookland Park Boulevard and Chamberlayne Avenue, the Willow Lawn Shopping Center and Fire Station 8 in the 1000 block of Williamsburg Road. Henrico residents served by the city could get water at a county fire station.

But there was some humor in the disaster. One man had his power restored only to lose it when a kamikaze-prone squirrel got into the transmitter. Another man suggested mixing whiskey with the heavily chlorinated water, but then he quipped, "Why waste good whiskey?" Some people refused to leave their homes, preferring to ride out the flood by sitting on their roofs.

Vice President Spiro Agnew visited the city on June 28 for two hours. He observed the James River from a helicopter and listened to the concerns of the citizens who had experienced the devastation of the flood. He was amazed at the water level and promised the full support of the Nixon administration.

Unlike Noah's flood, this flood did not last for forty days. Within a week, Richmond was getting back to normal. Water was again fit for human consumption, bridges were reopened and people returned to work. However, normal included soldiers in the streets blocking access to various places, as well as helicopters flying overhead. But the cleanup was getting underway. Shovels and garden hoses were used to clean up the mess. The predication was that the cost of the flood would be in excess of $330,000,000, but not a life was lost in Richmond. There was a lot of misery, but no deaths.

Letters to the editor of the *Richmond Times-Dispatch* captured the mood of the people. Articles included: "Efforts of Many Eased Disaster"; "Thanks to Policemen Who Kept the City Safe"; "Lauds City Leaders for Meeting Crisis"; "Outstanding Work Done by Utilities"; and "Harness the James, Flood Victims Urge." In reviewing the correspondence, Richmonders were generally happy with the response of the city and the counties to the crisis.

And there was this editorial comment: "Agnes will live in the memories of those tens of thousands of persons left homeless." The United States Weather Bureau admitted, "A situation like this really brings home that while we may have the most modern technology when natures goes on a

The Richmond flood wall. *Photograph by Walter S. Griggs Jr.*

rampage, we are its prisoners. All you have to do is look at the situation here in the City of Richmond to see that the words 'prisoner of nature' is to be interpreted literally."

There is general consensus that Agnes brought the greatest flood Richmond had ever experienced, but there was no one alive to remember the flood of 1771, and in 1771, technology did not exist to provide accurate measurements of the floodwaters. But the good news is that a flood wall was built in Richmond in 1995, which might end the contest for the deepest flood to inundate Richmond.

There are no monuments to Agnes, just bad memories. However, the flood wall might be considered a monument since it exists because Agnes and other floods came to Richmond. Remember, we do not have Noah's rainbow, but we do have our flood wall.

## Chapter 2
# A TRAITOR BURNS RICHMOND
## 1781

Churches hold time within their walls. Parishoners and pastors may change, but the church building remains much the same. A visitor can walk into St. John's Church on Richmond's Church Hill, sit in a pew and reflect on March 23, 1775, the day on which Patrick Henry of Virginia spoke these famous words that ignited a revolution: "Is life so dear, or peace so sweet, as to be purchased at the price of chains and slavery? Forbid it, Almighty God! I know not what course others may take; but as for me, give me liberty or give me death!" Although most people recall this speech, few Richmonders know that St. John's Church was also near the possible site of a battle when the King's Army came to Richmond in 1781 to fight for "King and Country" and the colonists demanded "Life, Liberty, and the Pursuit of Happiness."

The impassioned words spoken in this Richmond church by Patrick Henry were followed by the War for Independence that began at Lexington and Concord, followed by an attack on Fort Ticonderoga. The capture of this fort is remembered by the demand of Ethan Allen to the British commander: "Surrender in the name of the Great Jehovah and the Continental Congress!" The Battle of Saratoga, fought in 1777, was where General Benedict Arnold was seriously wounded after showing great courage and ability in achieving victory for the Continental army. If Arnold had died at Saratoga, he would have been remembered as an American hero.

Arnold was one of George Washington's best generals, but his successes were not rewarded in the ways he deemed appropriate. He seemed to have felt unappreciated and was frustrated. While in command of the Continental army in Philadelphia, Arnold married a British Loyalist, Peggy Shippen, who seemed to have let her new husband know her negative feelings about the Revolution and her dislike of George Washington.

Following duty at Philadelphia, Benedict Arnold was given command of the fort at West Point, New York, which was an important assignment at a strategic location. At his new post, Mrs. Arnold arranged for her husband to meet a British master spy, Major John André, her ex suitor. After a meeting in July 1780, General Arnold wrote several letters offering to turn West Point over to the British for £21,000 sterling. At the same time, he began to weaken the defenses at West Point. In September 1780, General Arnold gave Major André the plans for the West Point fort.

Major André was caught with the plans by the colonial militia and was hanged as a spy. His last words were, "I pray you bear me witness that I met my fate like a brave man." The papers found on his person left no doubt that Arnold was a traitor.

Arnold escaped to the British forces, exchanged his blue uniform for the red one of a British brigadier general and was ordered to attack Virginia by the British commander in chief, Sir Henry Clinton. One historian suggested that "the defection of Benedict Arnold was followed, as is usual in such cases, by the display of an inordinate zeal in the cause of his new master." This was the first major campaign assigned to Arnold, and it took zeal. Arnold was on his way to fight his fellow countrymen in Virginia.

Governor Thomas Jefferson was unaware that twenty-seven British ships were on their way to Virginia from New York. By December 30, 1780, the flotilla had reached Hampton Roads. Arnold had under his command 1,600 troops, composed of the Edinburgh regiment under Colonel Dundas, the Queen's Rangers under Lieutenant Colonel Simcoe and a detachment of New York volunteers, as well as other units. Assigned to these units were these highly regarded officers who were probably appointed to watch General Arnold, since traitors sometimes do not have the best reputations for loyalty.

From Hampton Roads, the ships sailed up the James River, and the soldiers destroyed some plantations along the way. On January 4, 1781, the army landed at Westover Plantation, where the officers were served a meal by Mrs. Mary Byrd. Her first cousin was Peggy Shippen, who had married Benedict Arnold. There was some evidence that Mary Bryd might have been a Tory sympathizer.

The invasion was a shock to Jefferson and the people of Virginia. They were not prepared to resist General Arnold and his army. But Jefferson worked furiously to get public supplies out of Richmond to prevent their capture before the British could seize them.

Facing no resistance, Arnold's army prepared to march to Richmond, which had been Virginia's capital for only a couple of years and could be described as a village. In response to the attack, Governor Thomas Jefferson, having now been warned of the British presence by General George Washington, called out the Virginia militia.

The British probably came to Richmond by following Route 5 and then marching down Main Street. Richmond was defended by about two hundred Virginia militiamen under the command of Colonel John Nicholas. The British attacked them near St. John's Church and on the hill at what is now Chimborazo Park on January 5. The terrain was described by Captain Johann Ewald, a Hessian soldier fighting for the British, as being "a very steep hill, overgrown with brushwood." Captain Ewald was assigned the task of capturing the hill. He wrote, "On the crest of the hill, I formed my men as quickly as possible in order to come up with the enemy, who had withdrawn to a wood behind a deep ravine. I deployed at once, formed two ranks well dispersed, and climbed up the hill. The enemy left after firing one volley." It was not a good day for the colonial army. At noon, Arnold's forces marched triumphantly into Richmond, "undisturbed by a single shot," while the colonial forces were running into the woods.

With no resistance, the British marched about eight miles west of Richmond to Westham under the command of Lieutenant Colonel Simcoe. There they burned the foundry, destroyed small arms and munitions and poured the gunpowder into the James River. They then returned to Richmond, where they indulged in drinking and general mischief.

After taking Richmond, General Arnold wrote Governor Jefferson a letter "offering to keep Richmond safe in exchange for all of the city's tobacco and other stores." A furious Jefferson, who had no intention of dealing with a traitor, rejected the offer. Accordingly, Arnold set Richmond on fire on January 6, 1781. Government buildings, as well as some private homes, were torched. Arnold also destroyed a lot of military stores. Even Captain Ewald, who fought with Arnold, commented, "Terrible things happened on this excursion; churches and holy places were plundered." A Connecticut paper reported as follows: "General Arnold obliged the inhabitants of Richmond to turn out all their rum, sugar, etc. into the street." Among the buildings burned were the public jail, some warehouses, and the ropewalk." There were reports that some hogs drank the rum that

The wooded area of Chimborazo Park where General Arnold's men charged into the Virginia militia. *Photograph by Walter S. Griggs Jr.*

was dumped in the street and got drunk. Have you ever seen a drunk hog? I have not, and I do not want to see one.

While his men were fighting and plundering, Arnold took up residence at City Tavern on the northwest corner of Ninth and Main Streets. Arnold's men set up camp around St. John's Church, and Governor Thomas Jefferson and most of Virginia's government officials fled to Charlottesville. W. Asbury Christian, in his book *History of Richmond*, wrote, "Arnold and his men, having pillaged, plundered, and burned much of the town, and fearing an attack, left Richmond about twenty-four hours after entering it." It was hard enough for Richmonders to see their city burned; but the fact that it was burned by a traitor made it unbearable. From Richmond, Arnold went back to Westover before returning to his base at Portsmouth.

Later, Arnold asked one of his officers what would happen if he (Arnold) were captured. The captain supposedly responded, "They will cut off your right leg, bury it with military honors [since it was badly wounded at Saratoga], and then hang the rest of you on a gibbet." General Washington,

Benedict Arnold. *Courtesy of the National Archives and Records Administration.*

however, gave orders to hang Arnold if he should be captured. Also, colonial marksmen were issued targets with Arnold's picture on them so they would know who to shoot.

Although Arnold was able to capture Richmond, his name became synonymous with treason. He was a traitor to his nation, and he went to England after the war. As he was dying, he said, "Let me die in this old uniform in which I fought my battles. May God forgive me for ever having put on another." Accordingly, it has been said that he was buried in the uniform of the Continental army. But the United States was unforgiving. Benjamin Franklin wrote, "Judas sold only one man, Arnold three million." Another man commented, "Arnold's actions are as black as hell." Obviously, nothing in Richmond has been named in Arnold's honor. Indeed, an unknown author wrote these lines:

*In fame's black roll, to latest times,*
*Shall Arnold's name be read;*
*Supreme in guilt, renown'd for crimes,*
*To every virtue—dead.*

Without question, most Richmonders would like to have seen him dead. He was trying to build his reputation as a British officer at the expense of Virginia's capital. Most assuredly, if he had been killed, he would not have been buried next to St. John's Church where Patrick Henry ignited the Revolution. I rather expect his remains would have been tossed into the nearest ditch.

# Chapter 3

# THE RICHMOND THEATER FIRE

## 1811

Thousands of Richmonders drive by the Monumental Church building at Twelfth and Broad Streets every day without being aware of its significance. The tragedy memorialized by this church building has faded from the memories of most people, and the building is no longer used as a house of worship. But it is still a sacred place that marks the site of the Richmond Theater, which was destroyed by fire on December 26, 1811, claiming the lives of seventy-two people whose remains are buried under the church and whose tragic deaths sent the entire nation into mourning.

In the days before movies, television and radio, the theater was an important source of entertainment for Richmonders. It was not unusual for actors and actresses to come from Europe and from across America to produce a play in the city. One of the best-known actresses to come was Elizabeth Poe, the mother of Edgar Allan Poe, who became a famous poet and author. In 1811, Richmonders attended the Richmond Theater that was located on the lot at H (Broad Street) and Twelfth Streets.

The first theater on the site was a renovated building that was used in the 1780s. The building was a frame, barn-like structure that had been used as a school. When the school moved out, it became a theater. It was called the New Theater, and the area was known as "Theater Square" or "Court's End." The first play in the new theater was *A School for Scandal*. In 1798, the building burned down and was replaced by a new theater in 1806, known as the Richmond Theater. The new theater was a small brick building and provided an intimate venue for theatergoers. Records indicate it was ninety feet in length, fifty feet in width and thirty feet high in front with room for offices. However, at least one actor considered it a poorly constructed theater and the worst theater the company had to use. The brick exterior of the building gave a false sense of security. Unfortunately, there were only three exits, narrow door frames, dark lobbies and winding stairways. Although it was a good place to see a play, it was a bad place to be in case of a fire because it was built at a time when there were no fire codes to protect patrons.

The night of December 26, 1811, was a time of festivity. It was the day after Christmas, and the Richmond Theater was filled with theatergoers. Many wealthy and distinguished Richmonders were in the crowd that filled the drafty building that night. One observer wrote, "Many young girls from Richmond's most affluent families were in attendance dressed in the dresses they had gotten for Christmas."

By the time the curtain went up, about five hundred men, women and children had filled the theater, which had an orchestra section, a huge performance stage, three levels of box seats and remote balcony seats. Ironically, the best seats for seeing a play were the worst seats in case a fire broke out and escape was necessary.

The playbill stated that the play was a benefit performance for Alexander Placide, a popular theater figure. The performance was originally scheduled for December 23 but was delayed due to the death of Elizabeth Poe. She was buried in the cemetery at St. John's Church in an unmarked grave. (The grave is now marked.)

The program for the evening included a French comedy entitled *The Father, or Family Feuds*, to be followed by *Raymond and Agnes*, or the *Bleeding Nun*.

The first play had finished and the audience was watching the last play of the evening, Matthew Gregory Lewis's pantomime *Raymond and Agnes*. But the audience never saw the end of the play. Before the second act, a stagehand was told to raise the chandelier, lit with candles, over the stage. The stagehand pulled the rope, which went through two pulleys. Slowly, the chandelier rose above the stage, and then the candles swung toward the highly flammable backdrop. Seeing the problem, an attempt was made to lower the chandelier, but the candles had set the backdrop on fire and then the fire reached the ceiling of the building and set it ablaze. In spite of the fire, the second act began.

As a costumed actor knelt before a painting of a woman on a curtain, flakes of burning material followed by showers of sparks fell on the stage. The actor saw the developing inferno and shouted, "The house is on fire!" Screams of "Fire! Fire! Fire!" echoed through the building. Within five

Richmond Theater fire. *Photograph courtesy of the Merritt T. Cooke Collection.*

minutes, the whole roof had turned into a sheet of flames. Fire bells began to ring as flames, choking smoke and burning material came down on the audience. With so many people and so few exits, the escape routes were soon jammed with terrified people who were blinded by the smoke. Within ten minutes, the entire theater was engulfed in flames, and over five hundred people faced death.

At least one of Richmond's fire engines responded, but it was useless. The firemen used "surround and drown" and did not enter the burning building. One witness said, "I did not see a drop of water poured on the fire." In 1811, Richmond relied on a volunteer fire department. One company was the Union Fire Company of Richmond. For equipment, the company used a hand-pumped engine and axes, ladders and hooks that the company maintained. When they responded, they could not help extinguish the fire since the fire was out of control. This was a battle that the firefighters could not win.

The panic of being trapped in the theater seized the audience, whose laughter turned to screams. The efforts to escape took many forms.

Many people tried to go down the stairs, but the stairs were soon jammed with people and escape was virtually impossible. People fell down and were trampled to death by those trying to escape. Clothes caught on fire and engulfed the wearer in excruciating pain. One woman was afraid to jump, and the crowd watched her burn alive. It was a sight no one would ever forget. Some people faced the prospect of either burning to death or jumping out of a window to the ground two or three floors below. If they jumped, some would be injured and some would be killed, but some would escape unhurt. The stench of burning flesh filled the night air. One woman was dragged out by her hair and another was covered by a man's overcoat after all of her clothes were burned off of her. Most people died from carbon monoxide poisoning and smoke inhalation.

Gilbert Hunt, a slave blacksmith, emerged as a true hero, as did Dr. James McCaw. Dr. McCaw led twelve women to a window and dropped them down to Gilbert Hunt, who caught them. After saving the women, Dr. McCaw jumped from the window. He survived but sustained permanent injuries.

Couples were found clinging to each other in death as they had in life. Sally Conyers and Lieutenant James Gibbon, her fiancé, went to the theater. He had left the theater but returned when he saw the fire. The two lovers died in each other's arms and were identified by her jewelry and by the military buttons on his uniform. They were a popular couple in Richmond, and their deaths were a tragedy.

Many of those who had escaped went back into the burning building to try to save a loved one only to lose their own lives. Governor George W. Smith escaped with his wife and then went back for his son. When he could not find his wife outside of the theater, he went back into the flames to look for her and was burned to death. His wife and son survived.

There are many contemporary accounts that capture the horror of that December night in Richmond. In a sermon, Reverend John D. Blair said, "And from those who escaped from the house or ran thither upon the alarm of the Bells, you heard frantic cries, the anxious inquiries. Where is my wife? Where is my husband? Where is my child? Where are my parents? And from some, already fatherless, Where is my dear mother?"

The *Richmond Enquirer* reported, "Women with disheveled hair; fathers and mothers shrieking out for their children; husbands for their wives; brothers for their sisters filled the whole area on the outside of the building."

In his *History of Richmond*, Asbury Christian wrote:

> *The frantic screams of women and children for help, and the loud voices of men trying to direct their friends and loved ones to a place of safety,*

*combined with the awful crackle and roar of the fast devouring flames, made the former scene of beauty and mirth one of indescribable horror. The rushing crowd, crazed with fright, soon blocked the narrow stairway and lobbies, then those who found themselves shut within the seething cauldron of fire trod upon others in their frantic efforts to escape.*

A minister wrote:

*And how little thought* [was given to] *the fair one whose curls were adjusted—whose garments, costly and elegant, were disposed, so as to produce on the spectator, the most impressive effect, that those curls were, that same night, to be crisped with devouring flames, and those garments to be denied the service of a winding sheet.*

"I saw several persons falling from the windows in the street in full blaze," one observer wrote. Another man noted, "Many of the dead were found at the foot of the narrow, winding staircase, which led from the boxes, and in the lobby immediately below the boxes."

A newspaper editor who was in attendance wrote:

*How can we describe the scene? No pen can paint it; no imagination can conceive it. A whole theatre wrapped in flames…a gay and animated assembly suddenly thrown on the very verge of the grave…many of them, oh! How many, precipitated in a moment into eternity…youth and beauty and old age and genius overwhelmed in one promiscuous ruin…shrieks, groans, and human agony in every shape…this is the heartrending scene that we are called upon to describe.*

The fire burned through the night. By morning, only charred timbers, scorched bricks and burned bodies remained. Most of the casualties of the fire were women, and many were teenagers.

Amid the tragedy, there was some suspicion that the fire was part of a slave insurrection, but this was not true. However, one slave did comment that "the negroes in the neighborhood said they were glad that the people were burnt in Richmond and wished that all white people had been burnt with them—that God Almighty had sent a little Hell for the white people and that in a little time it would get greater."

The remains of the dead, rich and poor, slave and free, black and white, young and old, were placed in two mahogany boxes. Reverend Buchanan told of the joy of the theater and then he said, "It is now a funeral pyre! The receptacle of the relics of our friends; and in a short time a monument will stand upon it; to point out where their ashes lay." Then the boxes were slowly lowered into the theater pit and covered with dirt and cinders. An observer said, "The whole scene defies description. A whole city bathed in tears! How awful the transition on this devoted spot. A few days since, it was the theatre of joy and merriment—animated by the sound of music and the hum of a delighted multitude."

Reverend John Blair's sermon at a memorial service contained these thoughts, "Prepare to meet thy God, O Israel. In the memory of the oldest of us, there never has been a more awful warning of the uncertainty of human life than this which is given us now."

Following the disaster, Richmond's Common Council proclaimed a four-month prohibition on amusements, which ended Richmond's social season. Many cities joined Richmond in mourning the dead. The United States Congress, on behalf of the entire nation, wore black for a month and suspended all entertainment. People across the United States mourned the loss of seventy-two people. One of the greatest disasters for the young republic had happened in Richmond.

A committee headed by John Marshall raised the funds to build a church on the site of the theater. It was designed by Robert Mill, who

Monumental Church in 2015. *Photograph by Walter S. Griggs Jr.*

designed the Washington Monument and the building that became the White House of the Confederacy. The main part of the church building is an octagon covered by a dome. A spire was planned for the building, but it was never added.

Monumental Church held its first services on May 4, 1814. Those at the first service were mostly relatives of those who had died. And one of the children who worshiped in the new church was Edgar Allan Poe. In the center of the portico is a monument to those who died on the night when a fire lit up the skies over the city of Richmond, Virginia.

The next time you see Monumental Church, reflect on the wandering spirits of those who died on that horrible December night when a conflagration lit up the city and the screams of the dying were heard throughout downtown Richmond.

## Chapter 4

# UNDERGROUND EXPLOSIONS IN CHESTERFIELD COUNTY

## 1839 AND 1844

The official seal of Chesterfield County displays a coal miner leaning on his pick. This seal pays tribute to those who labored in the coalfields of the county during the early days of our nation's history. Although coal is no longer mined in Chesterfield, the rich and tragic history of coal mining must not be forgotten.

Coal was first mined in the county as early as 1730 following its discovery in the early 1700s. Chesterfield coal was used to supply the fuel to make cannons during the American Revolution, and Thomas Jefferson stated that the quality of Chesterfield coal was excellent and used it to heat the White House. Eventually, streetlights in New York, Philadelphia and Boston were fueled by Chesterfield coal.

Mining methods went through somewhat of an evolution in the county. It began in Chesterfield with digging shallow pits or trenches to reach the coal; later, inclines were dug to reach the coal deposits to a depth of about two hundred feet. By the mid-1700s, deep shafts had been dug that were supported by timbers or brickwork. These Chesterfield mines were the first commercial mines in the United States. By one count, "there were hundreds of drill holes, shafts, slopes and open pit mines in the Midlothian area of Chesterfield County."

Picks and shovels were used to mine the coal. The coal was then tossed into baskets, hauled to the surface by mule or steam power and then shoveled on to railroad cars or into wagons pulled by mules and carried to Richmond. In some cases, mules worked in the mines. Many of these mules were born

The seal of Chesterfield County, Virginia, showing coal miners. *Courtesy of Chesterfield County.*

in the mines and lived their entire lives without seeing daylight. Midlothian Turnpike (Route 60) was constructed for wagons to carry coal from Chesterfield to the docks in Richmond. Later, a railroad was built to carry the coal. It was the second commercial railroad constructed in the United States and was named the Chesterfield Railroad.

Slaves, who were rented out by their owners, and free blacks did most of the hard labor under the supervision of white managers. A slave made thirty dollars a year, received a suit once a year and had a month's vacation at Christmas. The mines were worked twenty-four hours a day in twelve-hour shifts.

Miners came from England to the county because of the pay and the availability of jobs. They settled in and around Midlothian. By the eighteenth century, there were numerous coal mines in the county. One of the largest in the Midlothian area was known as the Black Heath Mine. It was one of the seven or eight active mines in the area, and together they were producing over a million bushels of coal annually.

Coal mining began in the Black Heath Mine in 1785, and the work was dangerous, unhealthy and dirty. Indeed, accidents were routine at a time when safety was not a primary consideration and first responders did not exist. If there was an accident, the miners and supervisors responded to render what aid was possible. Explosions, cave-ins, asphyxiation, being hit by a pick, gas, flooding, disease and coal dust were only a few of the hazards associated with mining. Although it is not known if they were used in the Black Heath Mine, some miners carried caged canaries into the mine. If there was gas in the mine, the canaries would die, giving the miners a chance to escape.

On March 18, 1839, about forty men, most of them slaves, were killed in a seven-hundred-foot shaft at the Black Heath Mine due to a violent gas explosion. The *Richmond Enquirer* published the following story: "We have not been able to ascertain the melancholy particulars of the blowing-up of the Black Heath Coal Pits. We only hear that the accident arose from inattention in not closing the door to a shaft, by which the fire damp [flammable gas found in coal mines] escaped and penetrated to other parts of the mine."

Of the men working in the mine, only two, who happened to be at work in crevices near the mouth of the shaft, and a third, who was maimed, managed to escape alive. This third man was on his way down the mine shaft in a basket at the time of the explosion. He was thrown one hundred feet into the air and landed seventy or eighty feet from the entrance and broke both legs and arms.

Every effort was made to get the bodies out of the pit where the miners had died like rats, but there was no hope of saving anyone. One can only imagine the horrors these miners faced when the mine exploded and trapped them. They knew they were going to die. Hopefully, death was swift.

Another article in the *Alexandria Gazetteer* reported that "the air in the mine was so impure that great caution was necessary to preserve the lives of those who descended to succor the unfortunate beings." In a follow-up story, the *Richmond Enquirer* stated, "The explosion took place in a shaft seven hundred feet deep, which was believed to be the deepest in the United States." The paper then reported that the "explosion was one of a most violent nature." One report said that the "explosion was so powerful as to blow pieces of timber out of the shaft to a distance of a hundred yards from it and rocked the countryside for miles around." A mining authority surmised, "Many survived the explosion of the inflammable gas but were destroyed by inhaling the carbonic acid which succeeds it. This death is said to be very pleasant; fairy visions float around the sufferer and the sufferer drops into the slope of eternity like one passing into delightful dreams." I guess there is some consolation in dying peacefully watching fairies as opposed to watching tons of coal fall down on you and knowing that you will die.

Various reports continued to focus on the tragic loss of life and the explosion. One newspaper reported, "Coal was blown out of the mine as were some miners. How it happened there is no telling. It is the general opinion, that one of the 'coasts' [passages for the air from chamber to chamber] must have been closed and that the 'inflammable gases accumulated to such an extent as to produce the explosion soon after miners entered the pit." Another theory was that a lamp designed to detect gas in the mines malfunctioned and caused the explosion." In the language of the times, the paper reported that all of the laborers were colored men and that some might have escaped death by visiting their wives at distant plantations and had not yet entered the pit. No one will ever know for sure how many miners were buried in the explosion, perhaps wielding their picks in a futile effort to save themselves. Their names have been lost to history.

A newspaper illustration about the Midlothian Coal Mine explosion. *Author's collection.*

On June 15, 1844, there was another major explosion that killed about a dozen men in the Black Heath Mine. The *Alexandria Gazetteer* reported that "at the time of the accident, we learned there were 12 hands in the pit: 8 colored men and 4 Englishmen." All of the African Americans were slaves. Although one man was saved, fallen timbers blocked the place where the accident occurred. The *Richmond Whig* ran a headline: "Terrible Accident." The paper reported that "a barrel of gunpowder was first ignited, and its explosion fired the gas, which was secreted." Although one man was pulled out alive, the rest of the bodies were found "horribly disfigured." The paper closed its story by reporting:

> *The explosion, as far as we can learn, was caused by the most wanton negligence on the part of unhappy persons, or the principal man among them. The funnel, used for ventilating the shaft, was stopped up so that a current of air could not pass through the works. In this situation, and while the…[vents] were filled with the inflammable gas, a blast was set off by some of the hands engaged in blasting coal. As might have been expected, a tremendous explosion followed.*

The company management worked for almost twenty-four hours to recover the bodies.

This second explosion closed the mine. For almost one hundred years, it remained closed until there was an effort to reopen the coal mining industry in the late 1930s. The effort did not succeed, and the Chesterfield mines are still filled with coal and the remains of those who tried to mine it.

The Black Heath Mine operated at a time when there were few safety devices. A miner going into a shaft had no assurance that he would ever see the light of day again. But the deaths of over three hundred miners helped to develop Chesterfield County. When you drive down the Midlothian Turnpike, remember you are driving on a road that was built to carry coal mined by men who did a dangerous job that helped to develop this nation. Whenever you look at the Chesterfield County seal, remember the men who mined the coal that fueled a nation.

## Chapter 5

# EXPLOSION ON BROWN'S ISLAND

## 1863

B rown's Island is a manmade island named for Elijah Brown. It is located in the James River at the end of Seventh Street. In the 1850s, it was a home for ducks, geese, turtles and other wildlife. Today, it is a popular venue for various concerts and entertainment activities. But this was not the case during the Civil War. In 1863, it was the site of the Confederate States Laboratory, which produced ammunition, friction primers, percussion caps and other ordnance for the Confederate army.

On Friday, March 13, 1863, Mary Ryan, an eighteen-year-old Irish woman, left her father's house on Oregon Hill and went to work in the laboratory on Brown's Island. She was one of several hundred young women who worked there and one of the most experienced. Most of the young women were between the ages of twelve and twenty, with one as young as ten. Young women were perfect for this type of work since it required small hands and nimble fingers to work with the ammunition. Also, they had to work to support their families since the men were serving in the Confederate military. Not many men worked in the laboratory, except as supervisors.

Mary Ryan sat at a table filling friction primers, which were used to ignite the gunpowder in a weapon to cause it to fire. This was dangerous work, and the workers were constantly reminded to be careful. Shortly after 11:00 a.m., Mary Ryan noticed that a primer had gotten stuck in a board; and in violation of all safety rules, she struck the table three times with the board to dislodge the primer. With the third strike, the primer ignited, and the resulting explosion sent her flying upward to the ceiling. The first explosion ignited other materials in the room, causing a second, much larger explosion that completely destroyed the building and shot Mary Ryan back into the ceiling. Mary Ryan had caused the worst explosion in Richmond's homefront during the war.

Richmonders heard a "dull and heavy explosion coming from the direction of the Confederate Laboratory Works" followed by dense smoke. Immediately, family members and other Richmonders rushed to the laboratory to see what had happened. The growing crowds could see the destruction, the smoke, the fire and the smell of the burning wood and flesh. Family members were desperate to determine the fates of their loved ones. Newspapers reported that "the explosion was found to have occurred in the room used for breaking up condemned cartridges. The walls of the building were forced outward and the roof fell in crushing sixty or seventy women." The *Richmond Examiner* reported, "The apartment in which the explosion occurred, about fifty feet in length and twenty feet in width, was blown into a complete wreck, the roof lifted off, and the walls dashed out, the ruins falling upon the women, and the horrors of fire were threatened to be added to those of the explosion; but the flames were suppressed." Male employers made valiant efforts to save those who had been injured by removing them from the building in spite of excruciating pain each movement caused them. The *Richmond Examiner* reported, "No sooner was one helpless, unrecognizable mass of humanity cared for and removed before the piteous appeals of another would invoke the energy of the rescuers since the injured could not move." Because the fire was so intense, some women jumped into the James River even though they could not swim, while others were horribly burned when their clothes caught fire along with their hair. Many were already dead while others were taken to General Hospital 2 on Seventh Street or to their homes.

A reporter wrote, "The shrieks of the wounded and plaintive moans of the dying, together with the agonized, tormented looks of those who had relatives on the island, rendered it a scene not likely to be forgotten." The *Richmond Examiner* reported, "Some ten to twenty women were found dead and from twenty to thirty were still alive, but suffering the most terrible agonies. They were blind from the burns, with their hair burned from their heads, and clothes hanging in burning shreds about their persons. Some of the young women were "burnt from head to foot, others were burned in the face and eyes, some had an arm or a leg divested of flesh and skin, others were bleeding with wounds received from falling timbers or in the violent concussions against floor and ceiling which ensued." The descriptions were almost too graphic to read.

The immediate treatment for the burned victims was the removal of their burned clothes and covering the body thickly with flour and cotton saturated with oil; chloroform was also administered. One can hardly comprehend the agony these young women must have suffered as life slowly passed away without the benefit of modern medicine.

A Confederate war clerk, John Jones, wrote in his diary, "Today a great calamity occurred in this city. In a large room of one of the government laboratories an explosion took place, killing instantly five or six persons and wounding, it is feared fatally, some thirty others. Most of them were little indigent girls."

Citizens organized clothing drives and collected food for those in need. They also collected other necessities, as well as money, and a dance was held to raise additional funds.

On a daily basis, death notices were published in the paper. One of those who died was Delia Clemens, and her family wrote this poem:

> We stood around Delia's dying bed,
> We saw her blue eyes close,
> While her heart the pulses fled,
> And from her cheek the rose.
> And still her lip in fondness moved,
> And still strove to speak
> To the mournful beings that she loved,
> And yet she was too weak;
> Till at last from her eye came one bright ray
> That bound us like a spell,
> And as her spirit pass'd away
> We heard her sigh—"farewell."

The obituary for Bridget M. Grimes included "in the death of this young girl, her circles of friends have lost a bright ornament. She was gifted with beauty of body and mind and possessed of a loving disposition, which won her the devotion of an immense number of friends." Although around forty-five women died, only three men were killed. One was John Woodcock, a sixty-three-year-old Methodist minister and a supervisor at the plant. He was highly regarded as an "exemplary man in all the relations of life."

Josiah Gorgas, chief of ordnance, interviewed the dying Mary Ryan and wrote this official account of the explosion: "The primer had stuck in the varnishing board and she struck the board three times very hard on the table

The unmarked grave of Mary Ryan in Hollywood Cemetery. *Photograph by Walter S. Griggs Jr.*

to drive out the primer. She says she was immediately blown up to the ceiling and on coming down was again blown up." Mary did not try to conceal what she had done. Why did she do such a careless act? Perhaps she was tired, frustrated and bored or had become careless from doing such routine work.

One woman who did not die was interviewed by the local paper. The paper described her as having her hands and face covered with cruel scars. She then added that for "five weeks nobody thought I would live. But I didn't mind it for it was in a good cause." Like a good soldier, she had fought for her nation.

Over forty-five people died in the explosion. Most were buried in unmarked graves. Reverend John Woodcock was one of the few people buried in a marked grave.

Mary Ryan rests in an unmarked grave in Hollywood Cemetery. She died in her father's house on nearby Oregon Hill. Only an occasional bird or squirrel visits her grave.

Recently, a stone marker has been placed in Oakwood Cemetery recognizing the sacrifices of the young women who died making ammunition not unlike what Rosy the Riveter would do in another war in the distant future.

## Chapter 6

# THE BATTLE "MID THE PINES OF RICHMOND'S HILLS"

## 1864

For generations, students at the University of Richmond have sung their alma mater, which begins with the phrase "Mid the Pines of Richmond's Hills." Yet these students probably do not know that a skirmish fought on and near the campus on the pine-covered hills saved Richmond from destruction and probably prolonged the Civil War.

Planning began in Washington, D.C., in early 1864, when President Abraham Lincoln approved a plan for a daring Union raid on Richmond with the objective of freeing the Union prisoners on Belle Isle. There was also evidence that the Federals planned to burn the city and kill Jefferson Davis, the president of the Confederacy, along with his cabinet. Since it was believed that Richmond was not well defended, the audacious plan had an excellent chance of success, which would hasten the end of the war.

The raid was led by General Judson Kilpatrick and Colonel Ulric Dahlgren. Colonel Dahlgren, the son of a Union admiral, was a war hero who had lost a leg in an engagement shortly after the Battle of Gettysburg. As the Federal cavalry came close to Richmond in the final days of February 1864, General Kilpatrick detached Colonel Dahlgren and ordered him to lead a force of over four hundred men along River Road, ford the James River, then recross the James River, attack Richmond from the south and liberate Belle Isle. At the same time, General Kilpatrick was to attack Richmond from the north along what is now Brook Road.

Realizing the difficulties of the mission, Colonel Dahlgren sought to inspire his men. His written comments included the lines, "You have been selected to attempt a desperate undertaking—an undertaking, which if successful, you will write your names on the hearts of your countrymen in letters that can never be erased and will cause the prayers of our fellow soldiers now confined in loathsome prisons to follow you and yours wherever you may go."

As Dahlgren's column of men in blue galloped along roads and cow paths toward Richmond, the colonel secured the service of Martin Robinson, an African American, to lead the cavalry to Dover Mills, a place where it was believed the James River could be forded. Unfortunately for the Union soldiers, the river was swollen and impossible to cross. Furious and believing his guide had betrayed him, the colonel hanged him from a tree before continuing toward Richmond.

Dahlgren halted his men about twenty miles west of Richmond at Sabot Hill in Goochland County, the home of Confederate secretary of war James Seddon and his wife, Sallie Bruce. The exhausted colonel knocked on the heavy front door of the old Virginia mansion and was greeted by Mrs. Seddon. After the colonel introduced himself, Mrs. Seddon said, "Your father was an old beau of mine in my girlhood days when I was a schoolmate

The state historical marker marking Dahlgren's raid. *Photography by Walter S. Griggs Jr.*

of your mother's in Philadelphia." Quickly, Mrs. Seddon obtained some 1844 blackberry wine, and the colonel and his father's former girlfriend started to enjoy the wine.

Before long, Colonel Dahlgren "was converted into an amiable guest, whose brain was soon exhilarated with the sparkling wine, and his manly soul was captivated by the gracious diplomacy and finesses of his father's former sweetheart." But not all residents were sipping wine and reminiscing.

The Union bugle call of "Boots and Saddle" had alerted the Goochland residents that the Federal forces were in the area. Learning this, two Confederates—General Henry A. Wise, a former Virginia governor, and Plumer Hobson, his son-in-law—mounted their fastest horses and galloped toward Richmond. Like the Revolutionary War hero Paul Revere, they were determined to alert Richmonders that a Union attack was imminent.

Responding to the news of the Union advance, the bell in the Capitol Square Bell Tower sounded the alarm, and frightened Richmonders filled the streets in search of news. The Confederate Armory Battalion, along with other units, were mustered into service and marched down Franklin Street to meet Dahlgren's men.

Meanwhile, Colonel Dahlgren left Sabot Hill and his charming hostess and headed toward Short Pump. After resting at Short Pump and feeding the horses, the colonel led his forces down Three Chopt Road toward Westham Plank Road (now Cary Street Road) on a cold, icy, rainy day. It was March 1, 1864.

There are a number of accounts of what transpired next, but there seems to be a consensus that there were two significant engagements between the Union and Confederate forces, along with intermittent skirmishes. The first clash was in the area of the present campus of the University of Richmond at around 5:00 p.m. According to one account, the Union command galloped up a road behind the present location of the University of Richmond Library and up the hill where Bostwick Lane now passes.

Dr. Frederic William Boatwright, president of the University of Richmond, stated that the initial encounter took place behind his home on Bostwick Lane. Then the fighting continued along Three Chopt Road to Mr. Benjamin Green's redbrick farmhouse, located at what is now 6510 Three Chopt Road.

In the first engagement, Lieutenant Samuel Harris of the Union army gave these commands, "Draw saber, forward march, trot, charge." The Confederate forces were soon overwhelmed and gave way in the face of the Union cavalry charge. The Union army continued to advance toward Richmond with victory in sight.

Fortunately, government clerks under the command of Captain John A. McAnarney were waiting for the Union cavalry on the Westham Plank Road, about five miles from Capitol Square near the Hicks Farm. Seeing the Confederates, Dahlgren's troopers screamed, "Charge the rebels! Cut them down!" A Confederate commented, "On they came like maddened fiends, but our splendid volley was too much for them."

Reeling from the gunfire and believing they were facing a major Confederate force, the Union bugler sounded retreat, and the Federal forces broke off the engagement and retreated back down Three Chopt Road. A defense force of old men, young boys and convalescing veterans had stopped the best the Union army could send against them. Richmond was saved. Mr. Green's house, around which the battle was fought, became a field hospital for the Union wounded and dying.

Just as Dahlgren was halted on Three Chopt Road, Kilpatrick was stopped on the north side of Richmond. The attacks, which could have captured Richmond and wiped out the Confederate government, had failed.

Desperately, Dahlgren and Kilpatrick sought to escape the surging Confederate forces. While General Kilpatrick returned to safety, this was not the case of Colonel Dahlgren. A day after the skirmish, Dahlgren was ambushed and killed in King and Queen County, Virginia. He was only twenty-one years old.

Papers found on his body outlining the mission of killing the Confederate president and other atrocities aroused a furor in Richmond. The authenticity of the papers remains a subject of scholarly debate even today.

There was no debate, however, among Richmonders who had been saved from the raid. Judith McGuire commented, "Richmond was safe and we felt no alarm." Another Richmond lady, Sallie Putnam, wrote, "What might have been was so terrible to reflect upon that it awakened grateful prayers for a merciful and protecting Providence."

## Chapter 7

# THE GREAT RICHMOND FIRE

## APRIL 1865

Richmond, Virginia, and Rome, Italy, have a lot in common. They are both allegedly built on seven hills, and they were both destroyed by fires set by their own citizens. Rome burned in 64 CE and Richmond in April 1865.

April 2, 1865, was a Sunday, and Richmonders flocked to their houses of worship. Churches are places of prayer, and those caught up in the Civil War needed to pray. The prayers offered over time have changed to meet different needs, but the prayers on this Sunday morning focused on the plight of the Southern Confederacy and on loved ones in uniforms of gray.

During the Civil War, St. Paul's Episcopal Church was known as the Cathedral of the Confederacy because of the large number of Confederate leaders, civil and military, who worshiped there. The faithful gathered on this Sunday. A lady commented that it was the kind of day "when delicate silks, that look too fine at other times, seem just to suit; when invalids and convalescents venture out into the sunshine." One churchgoer declared that the "Sunday was a fair, spring day. The trees in Capitol Square across from St. Paul's were quickening from bud to leaf. Church bells rang out their admonition to cease labor and come to worship." No one knew that this beautiful Sunday would be the day when old Richmond died and many lives would be changed forever. It would be the day when a conflagration engulfed Richmond, and the Union army, in a twist of fate, would rescue the city from destruction.

Among those going to St. Paul's that beautiful Sunday morning when the leaves were turning green, the squirrels were scampering up the trees and the birds were singing was Jefferson Davis, the president of the Confederacy. He walked down the center aisle and sat in his usual pew. Because of the threat that the Union forces might capture Richmond, the president's wife, Varina, had left town. The president worshipped alone, but the church was filled with the ladies of Richmond, who were dressed in mourning attire to show their grief over the loss of loved ones. Also in attendance were Confederate military officers and other high-ranking government officials.

It was communion Sunday, and the Reverend Doctor Charles Minnigerode, a German immigrant who still spoke with a German accent, was aware of the anxiety that filled his congregation. According to many churchgoers, he read Habakkuk 2:20: "The Lord is in his holy temple; let all the earth keep silence before him." As he prepared to offer communion, the sexton, William Irving, walked down the center aisle, touched President Davis on the shoulder and handed him a note. Immediately, the president read the note, got up and left the sanctuary. It was said that he turned ashen and walked unsteadily out of the church. This is understandable since the note advised him that the Confederate defenses at Petersburg had broken and that the Confederate government must abandon Richmond and head to Danville, Virginia. The Union army was headed toward Richmond with no Confederate forces to stop them. Richmond was to be abandoned to the enemy.

It was not unusual for the president to leave during a service, but when the sexton brought more messages and other Confederate officials started to leave, the congregation got uneasy, and rightfully so. In spite of the rector's request for the members to stay, many members of the congregation began to leave. When the sexton appeared the fourth time, people left the church en masse. One parishioner said it would have been easier to stop Niagara Falls than to keep people from leaving the church.

Down the street at Second Presbyterian Church, the church where General Thomas J. "Stonewall" Jackson had worshipped, the Reverend Doctor Moses Hoge was preaching when a messenger gave him a note informing him of the imminent fall of Richmond. Dr. Hoge said:

> Brethren, trying times are before us. General Lee has been defeated; but remember that God is with us in the storm as well as in the calm. We may never meet again. Go quietly to your homes, and whatever may be in store

*for us, let us not forget that we are Christian men and women, and may the protection and blessing of the Father, the Son and Holy Ghost be with you all.*

As the congregations left their churches, they met members of other churches along Grace Street and shared the news of what they had seen and heard. They had no idea how the Union army would treat the inhabitants of a city that they had been trying to capture for over four years.

In contrast to the concern of the members of the white congregations, members of black congregations were smiling. They were looking for the Union army that would bring them freedom and end their enslavement. To these people, the men in blue were their saviors and not their conquerors. They began to sing, "Slavery chain done broke at last; slavery chain done broke at last—I's goin' to praise God 'til I die" and "John Brown's body lies moldering in the Grave."

In response to the emergency and to meet the financial needs of the people, the banks opened their doors at 2:00 p.m. so people could withdraw their money. Some people packed their money into barrels to be carried to safety. And people going to the banks could see documents burning near government buildings and in Capitol Square. Some of the documents were being burned because they contained evidence that could lead to executions; therefore, they had to be destroyed. But their destruction was also a signal to Richmonders that the invading Union forces were near at hand and that the Confederate government was in chaos.

By Sunday afternoon, the leadership of the Confederacy was meeting to plan the evacuation of the city, to save the people from the assumed vengeance of the Union army and to make an effort to preserve the Confederate government by moving it to Danville. In the afternoon, Mayor Joseph Mayo told city council that the Confederate government was departing. Pursuant to plans, the council appointed committees to destroy all of the alcoholic liquors. This was mandated "to prevent disorder resulting from the intoxication of the troops of either army, as well as Richmonders."

While the city was preparing for the invaders, President Davis left his home when a carriage arrived for him, and he headed for the depot to board a train for Danville. Trains were lined up at the station to head for Danville with government officials, Confederate gold and the military. Some citizens were also trying to escape, but there was a lack of transportation. Thus, Richmonders were being abandoned to their fate. They were trapped in a dying city.

The train carrying Davis left Richmond around 11:00 p.m., crossed the James River on the railroad bridge and left the Confederate capital about twelve hours from the time he had entered St. Paul's to worship. From the train, the president could see the burning documents, the people filling the streets and the capitol building designed by Thomas Jefferson still flying the Confederate flag. The evacuation continued well into the night.

After dark, the destruction of the whiskey began. Whiskey barrels were broken open and their contents dumped into the street; bottles full of whiskey and kegs of whiskey were emptied into the gutter. Although the whiskey was dumped into the street, men began to drink it. Some emulated dogs by lapping up the whiskey; others put it in their hats, boots and anything else that could hold liquor. The people who went for the whiskey were described as the "vilest of the vile." The *Richmond Whig* reported, "Drunk with vile liquor, the soldiers roamed from store to store on Main Street, followed by a reckless crowd as drunk as the soldiers. Confederate soldiers used the butts of their rifles to break into jewelry stores, clothing stores, boots and hat stores, and confectionary stores." These stores were objects of special attraction to the pillagers.

In addition to taking the liquor, the citizens also helped themselves to all kinds of supplies and food from the commissary warehouses that were opened so the citizens could take the food instead of letting the Union army get it. The contents were quickly scooped up. Richmonders were prowling the streets collecting supplies, drinking whiskey and looting the shops.

The proud capital of the Confederate States of America was desecrated. It was filled with looters and left to the Union army, which had been mounting "On to Richmond Drives" since 1861. Only a few Confederate soldiers remained to protect the people. These soldiers, as well as the citizens, were largely ignorant of what was about to happen to them and their dying nation.

On the morning of April 3, Richmond's mayor, Joseph Mayo, received orders from Lieutenant General Richard S. Ewell to "fire the four principal tobacco warehouses of the city." The mayor knew the fires would spread and possibly destroy the business district of the city, but the Confederate leadership would not relent in its decision to burn the warehouses to keep their contents from the Union army. General Ewell was Richmond's military commander and was under orders to destroy the city's tobacco, cotton and other commodities before the Union forces could get to it. This decision was supported by President Davis.

The Confederate leadership believed that Richmond's well-organized, paid fire department with two steamers could fight the fire if it got out of control. Ewell asked the fire department to stand by in case it was needed. Unfortunately, Richmond did not have sufficient resources to control either the fire or the riots that accompanied it. It would have made more sense to throw the tobacco and other items in the nearby James River. This would have saved Richmond from a devastating fire, but this plan was rejected.

It was believed that the fires were set by Confederate authorities late on Sunday night. Fires were started in the Shockoe, Public, Mayo's and Dibrell's Warehouses and spread from the warehouses to homes, as well as to businesses. Some of the fires were started by drifting embers, paper torches or vandals. It was reported that two fires were started by mobs. It will never be known who set all of the fires, but a good guess is that mob rule took over, especially the prisoners who had been freed from the state penitentiary.

In the middle of the night, "a huge volume of smoke like an illuminated balloon shot high into the air followed by an explosion that shook the earth." This was the explosion of the CSS *Virginia II*, a Confederate ship. "The exploding ship sent flaming shells arching upward to burst in the sky," not unlike the "rockets' red glare" that exploded over Fort McHenry in the War of 1812. Other Confederate ships in the James River fleet were also blown

Richmond fire of 1865. *Courtesy of the Library of Congress.*

up, with the steel and wood flying like lethal missiles through Richmond. The Confederate fleet was in flames.

Judith McGuire, wife of Reverend John McGuire, "was startled by a loud sound like thunder; the house shook and the windows rattled, it seemed like an earthquake in our midst." There is a consensus that the greatest blast came from the magazine, which was located below the brick almshouse in the eastern end of the city. "Tombstones were overturned in Shockoe Cemetery. Thousands of window panes were blown out, doors of houses were torn off of their hinges and chimneys caved in; destruction was everywhere. The thunderous explosion might almost have awakened the dead. The earth seemed to writhe in agony."

In a few hours, there was another explosion, much louder than the first since it was closer to the center of the city. Houses and windows shivered all over Shockoe Hill. The armory had exploded. The lower part of the city was burning, and the streets were covered with broken glass. To add to the chaos, fire bells were ringing, train whistles were blowing and people and horses were running down the streets. Richmond was being destroyed by fires, explosions and mob rule.

There are many accounts of the fire. Not surprisingly, people place events at different times and have different memories of what happened. It was said that the fires were first seen to go straight up as they climbed the tallest buildings, then they spread out and engulfed more buildings. Ships were blown up, as were the arsenal and the armory. Mary Fontaine recalled, "Richmond was burning and there were no alarms…I watched those silent, awful fires; felt that there was no effort to stop them; but all, like me, were watching them, paralyzed and breathless." They could only watch their city turn to ashes while bricks and burning embers fell to the ground. Banks, hotels, churches, saloons, businesses, cherished possessions and homes were all engulfed in the flames.

The Confederates left Captain Clement Sullivan with the responsibility of burning the Mayo Bridge, the last bridge across the James River, after the last military units passed over it. This bridge was the last escape route from Richmond. As Richmond was engulfed in flames and explosions rocked the city, Sullivan was told that everyone had crossed the bridge and that he should "blow her to hell." He complied. As he rode across the burning bridge, he saw the Federals enter Capitol Square, "and then he turned and rode away."

With Richmond in flames and the people fleeing their homes and businesses, Mayor Joseph Mayo met the Union forces at the line of fortifications just beyond Tree Hill, near the junction of the Osborne Turnpike and New Market Road, around 7:00 a.m. He gave the Union officers this note:

*To the General Commanding the United States Army in front of Richmond:*

*The Army of the Confederate Government having abandoned the City of Richmond, I respectfully request that you will take possession of it with an organized force to preserve order and protect women and children and property.*

*Respectfully,*
*Joseph Mayo, Mayor*

Shortly thereafter, the Union forces entered the former capital of the Confederacy by riding down Main Street and into Capitol Square. The Union army musicians played "Yankee Doodle," "The Girl I Left Behind Me" and "Dixie" as they occupied the citadel of the Confederacy. A Union soldier commented, "Our reception was grander and more exultant than even a Roman emperor, leading back his victorious legions with the spoils of conquest, could ever know."

Richmonders gathered in Capitol Square to escape the fires. "Fathers and mothers, and weeping, frightened children sought this open space for a breath of fresh air." But the square was as hot as a furnace. The refugees from the burning city watched as the Confederate flag came down from the capitol to be replaced by Union guidons and the Stars and Stripes. The raising of the United States flag over the capitol building was not unlike the raising of the United States flag over Iwo Jima during World War II. And for the first time in four years, Richmonders listened to "The Star-Spangled Banner" being played. Emmie Sublett, a thirteen-year-old, wrote, "The Yanks came in…and first of all placed the horrible stars and stripes, which seemed to me to be so many bloody gashes, over our beloved capitol. Oh, the horrible wretches." But those "horrible wretches" saved Richmond.

General Godfrey Weitzel, who was in command of the Union soldiers, immediately ordered the fires to be extinguished. Moses Hoge's parsonage at Fifth and Main would have been lost to the fire but for the fact that the men poured water on it and put wet blankets on its burning roof. The Union forces also protected the home of Mrs. Robert E. Lee. Two fire engines owned by the city were used by the Union soldiers, but the intense heat drove the firefighters back from the roaring fire, and members of the mob cut the hoses. A large piece of burning coal fell on the steeple of the United Presbyterian Church on Shockoe Hill at the corner of Eighth and Marshall Streets. It burned so slowly that it could have been put out if anyone could have gotten to it, but it was not saved. The church, though it stood in a thickly populated part of the city, was the only structure that burned in that neighborhood.

It was said that "the city was wrapped in a cloud of densest smoke, through which great tongues of flame leaped in madness to the skies." Another comment was that "ten thousand shells bursting every minute in the Confederate arsenal and laboratories were making an uproar such as might be heard when all the world's artillery joined in battle."

To extinguish the fire, bucket brigades were organized, and the city's two fire engines were kept in service. The fires were finally extinguished

Home of Robert E. Lee's family in Richmond, which was saved from the evacuation fire. *Courtesy of the Library of Congress.*

A fire engine at the Richmond evacuation fire of 1865. *Courtesy of the Library of Congress.*

by pulling down threatened buildings to create a firebreak. This tactic was aided by a shifting of the wind. Weitzel recalled, "We found ourselves in perfect pandemonium. Fires and explosions in all directions; whites and blacks either drunk or in the highest state of excitement were running to and fro on the streets apparently engaged in pillage or in saving some of their scanty effects from the fire. It was a yelling, howling mob."

One writer commented, "The roaring, the hissing, and the crackling of the flames were heard above the shouting. The confusion of the immense crowd of plunderers, who were moving amid the dense smoke like demons, pushing, rioting and swaying with their burdens, made a passage to the open air. From the lower portions of the city, near the river, dense black clouds of smoke arose as a pall of crêpe to hide the ravages of the devouring flames, which lifted their red tongues and leaped from building to building as if possessed of demonic instinct and intent upon wholesale destruction."

The fires were contained by the afternoon of April 3, but there were still flare-ups. In addition to the damage caused by the fire, the streets were covered with broken glass, burned boards, broken furniture and fallen bricks. To save their furniture, many Richmonders put what was left in their front yards, and family treasures were hidden in various places. But Richmond's business district was burned out of existence.

Over nine hundred homes and businesses were destroyed, and many people were left homeless. Authorities claimed that "two distinct fires spread rapidly throughout the commercial and industrial sections of the capital. The core of the burned-out area, some 35 blocks, extended from the James River and in some areas as far north as Capitol Square and from Fourth Street east to Sixteenth Street." Fortunately, the Federals reinforced the Richmond fire brigade, fought the fire and kept it from extending beyond Seventh Street and Franklin Street. Fires were generally stopped by destroying buildings to create fire breaks.

Fires were still smoldering on April 4, when President Abraham Lincoln made a brief visit to the city and visited the White House of the Confederacy. He also toured the burned-out city. The former slaves greeted Father Abraham as the man who freed them from slavery. Lincoln lived to see his armies capture the Confederate capital, but his life was ended by an assassin's bullet before he could fulfill his promise of "malice toward none."

The *Richmond Whig* provided a summary of the state of Richmond following the fires and Federal occupation. The article read:

> *Yesterday afternoon* [April 5, 1865], *the Richmond Fire Brigade commenced the very necessary work of pulling down the toppling walls that overhang the avenues of the burnt district ready to descend any moment in an avalanche of brick, granite, and mortar upon the heads of the throngs of citizens and soldiers who are curious seekers among the ruins of once fair and beautiful Richmond. The military authorities, who gave the order for the demolition of the ruins, reinforced the Fire Brigade by a detail of colored troops, who worked manfully at the ropes.*

It was ironic that the capital city was set on fire by the men who were to defend it and saved from total destruction by United States troops. In fact, Union soldiers saved the capital of the Confederacy.

The window of Second Presbyterian Church that was put back in place in 1971 after having been in storage since 1865. *Photograph by Walter S. Griggs Jr.*

On April 9, General Robert E. Lee surrendered at Appomattox Court House. Richmonders were awakened by the salute of one hundred guns and whistles from every Union ship that had a whistle. The "cruel war" was over. The nation was reunited.

To capture the plight of Richmond, Reverend Minnigerode read these lines from Psalm 44:1 to his congregation at St. Paul's Episcopal Church: "Yea, for thy sake are we killed all the day long; we are counted as sheep for the slaughter.... For our soul is bowed down to the dust; our belly cleaveth unto the earth. Arise for our help, and redeem us for thy mercies' sake."

Richmond was still smoldering when General Robert E. Lee issued General Order Number 9, which reminded the Army of Northern Virginia, "You will take with you the satisfaction that proceeds from the consciousness of duty faithfully performed, and I earnestly pray that a merciful God may extend to you his blessing and protection." And General Lee and many soldiers came home to the city that they had fought to save only to find smoldering ruins.

Perhaps the last repair to fire-ravaged Richmond took place when the stained-glass window of the Second Presbyterian Church was put back in place. The window had been blown out during the explosion of 1865 and was stored in the attic for 112 years. In 1971, during the restoration of the church, the window was placed over the main entrance.

Today, visitors to Richmond can see a city that recovered from a fire that destroyed its business district, but there are still reminders of the fire in the form of historical markers and old buildings that survived the fire, including the Virginia State Capitol.

You can walk through Capitol Square and see the ghosts of frightened Richmonders, long-dead soldiers, women dressed in black and newly liberated slaves. But you will not see Ole Virginia—Ole Virginia died in the great fire of April 1865.

## Chapter 8

# DISASTER IN CAPITOL SQUARE

## 1870

For Virginians, and especially Richmonders, Capitol Square is a special place. The seat of the Virginia State government, the square's iron fences hold history. By walking through the square, you might see the governor, legislators, tourists, state employees, Capitol Police and, of course, pigeons and squirrels. Until an iron fence was installed around the square in 1819, it also was home to cows, pigs and sheep. There is something historic to see with every step a visitor takes. One can stand where Jefferson Davis stood to take the oath of office as president of the Confederate States of America, see where Robert E. Lee assumed command of the Confederate forces in Virginia, admire the Governor's Mansion or see the Bell Tower that was used to summon Richmonders in an emergency.

Designed by Thomas Jefferson, the cornerstone of the capitol building was laid in 1785 and the Virginia General Assembly met there for the first time in 1789, but the building was not finished until 1796. When completed, it housed the three branches of government: the legislative, the executive and the judicial. The capitol building was not only the home of the Virginia legislature, but it was also where the congress of the Confederate States of America met during the Civil War.

Unfortunately, this iconic building was the site of one of Richmond's greatest disasters when the floor of the room where the Virginia Supreme Court of Appeals met collapsed in what has become known as the Capitol Disaster. It occurred on April 27, 1870, and is frequently compared to the Richmond Theater fire of 1811 as one of Richmond's major disasters.

The genealogy of the Capitol Disaster can be traced to April 1861, when Confederate artillery fired on Fort Sumter off the coast of South Carolina. The shells that struck the fort plunged the nation into a great Civil War. From First Manassas, where General Thomas J. Jackson was said to stand "like a Stonewall," to the disastrous charge at Gettysburg and Lincoln's Gettysburg Address, the capture and burning of Richmond and the final surrender at Appomattox Court House in April 1865, Richmond was a central focus of the Civil War. During the conflict, the Union objective was to capture Richmond because it was the capital of the Southern Confederacy and the Capitol Building represented the Confederate government—Richmond was frequently referred to as the Confederate Citadel. Battlefields and cemeteries remain around Richmond for tourists to visit and reflect on the tragic conflict.

Following the end of the war, there was a period of Reconstruction when Union forces occupied Virginia in what was then known as Military District 1. Most Richmonders were humiliated by the years of Reconstruction that finally ended on January 26, 1870. The city was ready to rid itself of the Union army and its minions who occupied many of the government offices in the city. Richmonders wanted to put the war, Reconstruction and Union appointees behind them.

Once Virginia was back in the Union, the General Assembly of Virginia passed the Enabling Act on March 5, 1870. The act empowered the governor to appoint a new council for the city of Richmond to serve until July 1, 1870. Under this act, the governor of Virginia appointed new members of the council to replace those who had been appointed by the military commander, and the new council appointed Henry K. Ellyson as mayor. However, there was a problem: there were two mayors. The mayor selected by the Federal authorities, George Chahoon, would not surrender his post to Henry K. Ellyson, the mayor appointed by the newly formed council. Unfortunately for the citizens of Richmond, Chahoon continued to act as mayor. He claimed that the act permitting the election of Ellyson was unconstitutional; therefore, Ellyson was not the legal mayor.

Richmonders felt that "no man who ever lived in Virginia excelled Mr. Ellyson's high moral standing, or business integrity, and certainly he was not excelled by any in untiring usefulness." It was also said that Richmonders knew little of "Mr. Chahoon except that he was an adventurer from the North, who came here as a 'Camp Follower' with the Federal army, and that nine-tenths of the people of intelligence and worth wanted to get rid of him."

With two mayors, two city halls and two police forces, there were fights among them and chaos reigned. Chahoon's presence reminded Richmonders of the pain of Reconstruction. In fact, Richmonders had a very low regard for those Northerners who came south following the Northern victory. George Christian reflected the sentiment of many Richmonders when he wrote, "These carpetbaggers, scalawags, and other cormorants who flocked and feathered here, like the miserable vultures they were, seeking whom and what they might devour and who generally left their country for their country's good." Such was the opinion held of Mayor Chahoon. Christian suggested that Chahoon's supporters came from "Oakwood," "Hollywood" and "Shockoe," which were Richmond cemeteries. The two rivals finally agreed to have the matter decided by the Virginia Supreme Court of Appeals, which met in the Virginia State Capitol.

April 27, 1870, was the day the decision of the court would be handed down. The courtroom in the capitol was packed with citizens who wanted to hear the decision of the court of appeals in what was termed the Richmond Mayoral Case and was reported in 19 Grattan, page 673 of the *Virginia Reports*.

The large number of people in attendance to hear the verdict put a lot of weight on the courtroom floor, which had shown signs of warping and weakness for many decades. Suddenly, there were some loud cracking noises, the supports gave way and the floor of the courtroom fell into the Hall of the House of Delegates, which was located under the courtroom. Approximately 355 people tumbled into the House chamber forty feet below. One can only imagine what it feels like to be standing on a floor that suddenly gives way under your feet and you start to fall straight down.

The dead, the dying, the injured and the survivors were thrown to the floor of the House of Delegates; 62 people lost their lives in the collapse, and 251 were injured. Many who fell to the floor were saved because they fell among the dead bodies, which shielded them from the falling floor. Some were buried alive under the debris, and someone screamed, "Oh, grave, where is thy victory? Oh, death, where is thy sting?" Blood, crushed bodies, brains and plaster covered most of those who had fallen. Fortunately, the judge's bench and some offices did not collapse.

An old pamphlet provided this account of the disaster: "The bell had just tolled the hour of 11, and death-like silence reigned as the clerk entered and placed his books on the table. Two judges were in their seats, while the rest of the judges were in the conference room. Suddenly, a panel of ceiling fell, and then the girder gave way with an awful crash, and the spectators who were in the gallery of the courtroom fell to the main floor of the House of Delegates along with bricks, mortar, splinters, beams, iron bars, desks and chairs." It was reported that "in a few seconds fifty-seven souls were launched into eternity." Several more would die later in the day. There were many comments about the thick dust that came from the fallen plaster that made the building look like it was on fire. Survivors clung to the windows and pieces of timber protruding through the walls until help arrived. If the House of Delegates had been in session, the death toll would have been much higher because the delegates would have been crushed by the falling floor.

One man commented, "I was standing in the courtroom some distance beyond the center; I heard a low rumbling sound and the floor gave a sort of a jump; I felt myself sinking, and I turned and saw the gallery falling over. I thought it would catch me; fortunately, it missed me. I fell into the darkness below; I found a dead body laying [sic] on me, a wounded man under me, and another at my side."

W. Asbury Christian wrote, "Suddenly, at the center door under the gallery, there was a loud report like the explosion of a gun. All eyes were turned in that direction when instantly there was another loud report, and, to the horror of all, the gallery gave way, carrying the timbers overhead, and then the main floor went down with a terrific crash. With a stifling cloud of dust, there came a great wail of horror with the agonizing cries and shrieks of the wounded and dying. A large number clung to doors and windows and saved themselves from the awful ruin beneath. The bell in the Bell Tower sounded the alarm of fire, for many thought the capitol was on fire from the white dust that was pouring from the windows. The moans of the suffering and dying mingled with the shrieks of loved ones as they recognized the dead body of one dear to them."

Soon, the fire bells began to sound an alarm. In the firehouses, the firemen hitched their horses to the steam fire engines and responded to the capitol. Richmond had five fire stations with five engines and two truck companies. Firefighters entered the building by using ladders to reach the windows. Other citizens joined forces with the firefighters to save as many people as possible and to dig them from under the debris that was suffocating them to death. At a time when racial relations were strained, blacks and whites worked together to try to rescue people.

Hats and other garments from the dead and injured were piled in front of Washington's statue. The senate chamber was made into a temporary morgue, but it was not large enough, so most of the dead and injured were

The Capitol Disaster showing the death and destruction. *Courtesy of Virginia Commonwealth University.*

taken outside and placed on the ground. Every physician in Richmond responded to the disaster to render all possible aid, and wagons and other conveyances took the injured to their homes.

The *Native Virginian* newspaper, published at Orange Court House, Virginia, reported the story as follows:

> *About 11 o'clock…a dense crowd of people had assembled, and just as the justices were about taking their seats on the bench, the gallery, which was packed with human beings, gave way, and the living mass was precipitated forward into the center of the room, which was also crowded to its utmost capacity, which, under the additional pressure, fell in with a terrible crash, carrying with it the entire mass of people and burying them under its weight, in the Hall of the House of Delegates, below. The shrieks of the wounded and dying were most heartrending, and the scene for a short time was too painful to describe. There, piled under the great weight of the debris of the courtroom and adjoining offices, were buried hundreds of men, struggling for relief and suffering most intense anguish, crushed, and nearly smothered. The few moments that elapsed before assistance could be rendered seemed an age and no pen can depict the anguish of those moments.*

The reporter commented on the ringing of the fire bells that brought help for the injured, as well as people who wanted to know if their loved ones were alive or dead. It was difficult to tell who was alive or dead since the bodies were covered with dust that made recognition difficult. The reporter commented about a man who was having a conversation and then the floor collapsed and killed him. The reporter observed, "How forcibly was it brought to mind that in the midst of life we are in death."

The *New York World* called the collapse "The Richmond Horror." The reporter wrote:

> *The sun rose bright and cheerful this morning over a city full of happiness which by midday was turned into mourning and desolation. One of the most frightful and appalling catastrophes occurred at the Capitol building wholly without a parallel by which nearly fifty [sixty-two] lives were lost and as many were maimed, and this day is henceforth remembered as a day of horror and calamity in Richmond's history.*

The headlines of many of the nation's newspapers illustrated how the nation responded to the disaster: "Death-Stroke," "The Terrible Calamity,"

"Frightful Accident," "Richmond in Mourning," "The Great Horror," "Terrible Calamity in Richmond, Virginia" and "An Awful Crash."

As is always the case following a disaster, a cause is sought. In this case, it was believed that a "large girder which was under the partition between the clerk's office and the courtroom snapped in twain, and immediately afterwards the floor begin to cave." Someone located the broken girder and "found that it had been broken off just in the center. It was hewn timber, and just where it broke off was a cut, as if a workman, in hewing, had make [*sic*] a miscut and driven his adze into the wood about a quarter of an inch." Under this theory, some unknown worker's mistake caused a tragedy.

Another theory put forth was:

> *A floor was thrown across and thus two stories made of one. In doing this, the architects, instead of inserting the floor beams in the wall of the Capitol, rested them upon a ledge or offset in the wall, which projects not more than four inches, and on this frail support, timbers measuring at least two feet by eight or ten inches thick, were rested, the constant tendency of which was to press out the walls and lessen the support.*

Another writer wrote, "The ends of the floor beams were rested in small notches that were cut into the offset to accept the ends of the beams and were held in place by gravity." The new floor was supported originally by pillars, but they were considered unsightly and were removed. It was also remembered that for many years, the floor had been concave to an extent that was alarming, but familiarity, as usual, removed this doubt of its safety. For over thirty years, the floor had been sagging, and it was amazing that it held up as long as it did.

Everyone seemed to agree that poor construction, faulty design and the additional weight of so many people caused the floor to collapse, hurling everybody in the courtroom through the ceiling of the Hall of the House of Delegates to the ground level below.

The tragedy united the north and south in grief. Former enemies sent money to help those who needed it. Even trains coming into Richmond were draped in black, as were all buildings. Someone said, "It would seem as if this terrible accident had proved that one touch of Nature makes the whole world kin."

Wednesday, May 4, was named by the governor as a day of humility and prayer. All businesses ceased, and black crêpe was placed on many doors.

Houses of worship were filled with those who felt the pain of the tragedy. At the Beth Shalom Synagogue, the rabbi reminded his congregation:

> *The brilliant mind and the feeble intellect; the distinguished jurist and the humble artisan; the successful merchant and the sturdy laborer all shared our common fate, all were engulfed in common ruin. Neither age, station, or condition was taken into account, as if to show us how we all stand amid the uncertainties of this life and the necessity for timely preparation for that which is yet to come.*

The Catholic churches held Masses for the repose of the "souls of the victims of the late disaster." The rector of St. Paul's Episcopal Church said, "The Capitol of Virginia is the tomb of her children."

A number of members of the Virginia Supreme Court of Appeals attended the service at Second Presbyterian Church. The Reverend Dr. Moses Hoge made three points in his sermon: "First, We should humble ourselves in profound acknowledgment of God's power. His ways are mysterious. We can not comprehend them with our limited resources. The King of Glory cannot enter through the narrow inlets of our understandings. Second, it is natural to hope and anticipate, but the lessons of every-day life teach us how different are the results of tomorrow from the expectations of today, and what slight causes change the whole current of life. Third, the suddenness of such calamities should teach us to be sweet and tender in social and domestic intercourse. If we leave our houses with unkind words; we may never have the opportunity of healing the wounds we inflict…We should plant flowers in our homes, as well as upon the graves of the dead."

The Supreme Court of Appeals met again a few days later in the courtroom of the city hall and decided that the Enabling Act was constitutional and that Henry K. Ellyson was the mayor of Richmond.

The court incorporated an account of the disaster in its opinion. It wrote as follows:

> *At 11:00 o'clock* [two] *judges took their seats upon the bench, and the other judges were just about to enter from the conference room; and the whole assembly were waiting in silent and earnest expectation when there was heard first a crack; and then immediately a crash; and the floor of the courtroom to within four feet of the judges' seats and that of the clerk's office sunk down carrying with it the hundreds of persons upon it. The gallery flowed on the instant with the living load and then immediately fell the false*

*ceiling which had been put over the room with the plaster and timbers; floors and gallery and ceiling piled upon the bleeding and suffocating mass, which had been carried down into the room below.*

After many years, a modest plaque was placed in the Capitol. There were plans for a larger memorial, but they were never implemented. The plaque states:

*This tablet was erected under an act of the General Assembly of Virginia approved March 16, 1918—to mark the scene of the Capitol Disaster which occurred on April 27, 1870, when the floor of the courtroom of the Supreme Court of Appeals, which was then above this hall, fell resulting in the deaths of sixty-two and the injuring of two hundred and fifty-one other persons.*

The Virginia State Capitol still stands as a symbol of the commonwealth. Proposals to tear it down after the disaster were rejected. Only a plaque reminds people of that fateful day when the floor fell in and destroyed so many lives.

## Chapter 9

# THE JEFFERSON HOTEL

## 1901 AND 1944

*The Jefferson Hotel seems destined to become one of the great attractions of the
entire southland, and a powerful inducement to the great army of tourists to turn
their steps in the directions of this city so rich in historic associations.*
—Richmond Dispatch, *1895*

Whil hen Richmonders say, "the Jefferson," they mean the Jefferson Hotel.
The creation of tobacco baron and Richmonder Lewis Ginter, the
Jefferson is a Richmond treasure. To walk through its doors is to walk back
in time to the Gilded Age of the 1890s. By walking through its lobby, you can
walk where presidents walked, eat where movie stars ate and perhaps see the
ghost of Elvis Presley, who was a frequent guest at the hotel. You can even
walk up the staircase that legends suggest was the inspiration for the staircase
featured in *Gone with the Wind*. You can see the alligator statue that replaced
the live alligators that lived in a pool in the Jefferson until the last one, Old
Pompey, passed away in 1948. There are many alligator stories, including
one about a lady who put her feet on what she thought was a footstool only
to discover that it was an alligator. Fortunately, she saved her feet! It has even
been noted that the alligators would crawl out of their pool at night and
sleep in chairs.

In October 1895, the Jefferson opened, and the *Richmond Dispatch* carried
a series of comments, including the following: "It is a magnificent hotel," "It
is patterned after the Louis XVI style of architecture," "A most attractive
location, combining a hostelry for social and business interests alike and

splendid in every detail." "A magnificent dining room with seating capacity for three hundred" and "The Lobby and Office and Grand Staircase are first-floor features." A reporter wrote, "Everything connected with the house is a state of utter magnificence, and, as it now stands, the hostelry is the most complete and luxurious in the South and takes a place of honor of representative American hotels."

A central focus in the lobby was a statue of Thomas Jefferson by Edward Valentine. It was described in detail: "The figure is elegant and impressive and the posture easy and graceful…The right hand holds the paper [the Declaration of Independence] that was so mighty in the destiny of this great republic." The Jefferson statue would appear in the news in the years ahead.

Thousands of Richmonders visited the hotel the day before its formal opening. They commented on its beauty and the presence of alligators. One writer said, "No city was prouder of a noble building than Richmond was of the Jefferson."

Richmonders now had a hotel that had risen from the ashes of the destruction of Richmond following the Civil War. It was a building that everyone could take pride in and enjoy staying in. Even those who never entered the Jefferson felt that they were part of it.

Then disaster struck! On March 29, 1901, a major fire swept through the hotel. The newspaper reported, "The hand of misfortune has fallen heavily on Richmond. The Jefferson Hotel, the pride and the delight and the greatest architectural gem in the State has perished in flames and at this hour the indications are some nine-tenths of the exquisite structure are damaged beyond all hope." How did a fire start that destroyed such an icon? There are several stories about how the fire began.

One of the first reports was that the "fire seems to have started in a defective flue in the fourth floor blanket room. It was noticed about 11:00 p.m. when smoke was seen to issue from the blanket room." Another report said:

> *The fire originated in a closet on the fourth floor at the southeastern corner of the building. There were also reports that a bellboy suspecting electrical problems ran up the stairs to find smoke coming from the southeast corner of the fourth floor. The bellboy used the hotel's firefighting equipment in an attempt to extinguish the fire, and he felt that he had been successful in putting it out. But in fact, however, the blaze was spreading unseen between the ceiling and the floor above.*

The newspaper reported that defective insulation on a wire started the fire.

If all of the versions of how the fire started were analyzed, it would seem to be agreed that the fire originated in a closet apparently on the fourth floor at the southeast corner of the building around 11:15 p.m. Some officials believe that the real cause of the fire will never be known.

The first alarm went to Engine 7 at 910 Cary Street at 11:19 p.m. This was followed by a general alarm that brought every piece of fire apparatus in the city, which included eight engine companies and three truck companies. The horses that pulled the apparatus were well-trained to bring the equipment to the right place after charging down the street with the sparks shooting from their horseshoes striking the cobblestone streets. There is nothing more memorable than seeing a horse-drawn, steam fire engine spewing smoke while racing to a fire.

Upon arrival, the fire department had difficulty in locating the blaze because of the heavy smoke. A steamer and hose carriage had stopped at Adams and Franklin Streets. Smoke was seen coming from a window on the sixth floor of the Main Street side of the building. To get water on the fire, a rope was lowered from the floor on which the fire was discovered and attached to a hose nozzle and sections of hose. Rapidly, the hose was drawn upward to the eager firefighters anxiously waiting to use it on the fire.

Unfortunately, two firemen were trapped by the raging fire. One fireman was from Station 3 and one from Station 5. They escaped "like squirrels by sliding down the hose to the ground, and alighting safely upon the pavement uninjured." Other guests escaped the fire, but not like sliding squirrels. A traveling salesman escaped by running down the steps. He fell and broke his leg, but he survived. One lady was carried out of the burning building while still in her nightclothes, and other people escaped by going down the fire escape or a fire department ladder. It takes courage to come down a fire escape or a ladder from the fifth floor of a burning building.

One man's escape prompted considerable comments. The gentleman got out of the bathtub and strolled through the corridor to the Franklin Street entrance. His state of dress is unknown. Many guests stayed in their bathrooms and used wet towels to protect themselves until they were rescued by firefighters. There were cases where some people refused to leave their rooms in spite of firefighters banging on the door.

Fortunately, the Thomas Jefferson statue was saved by wrapping it in mattresses, tying ropes around it and dragging it out of danger. The head was broken off but was later repaired. Saving the statue was a major accomplishment.

Caroline with Thomas Jefferson in the lobby of the Jefferson Hotel. *Photography by Walter S. Griggs Jr.*

The water being poured on the fire seemed to have no effect. The fire continued to extend through the building even though the firefighters were doing all they could to save the hotel. Eight fire companies poured water on the inferno for hours in spite of blistering heat and choking smoke, yet the fire spread higher and higher as it consumed the hotel.

The firefighters on the Jefferson Street side poured in tons of water from all of their hose lines, while those who were on the Adams Street side were trying to stay the progress of the flames. "They got on the roof of adjoining property and directed immense streams on the walls of the building." Before long, a portion of the wall collapsed and fell to the ground, and the western clock tower soon crashed to the ground. The conflagration continued unabated as a Richmond treasure was being turned into ashes and rubble.

A reporter wrote, "The fire department fought with unwavering energy under the shadow of a lofty wall that threatened to totter and fall from the dizzy height of the roof of the unburning portion of the hotel and from the tops of adjoining residences from every point from which it seemed possible to throw a stream upon the leaping flames." It was reported that every trick known to firefighters of long experience was brought into use, but they failed. Only the Franklin Street front of the Jefferson and the power house were saved.

After an all-night battle, the fire was marked under control at 5:00 a.m. When Richmonders gathered to see their hotel, they saw smoke-grimed ceilings, destroyed furniture, collapsed walls and smoldering ruins to mark the place where the majestic hotel once stood.

It was observed that "these many streams of water seemed to have no effect whatever. If anything, the fire demon seemed to grow only more determined and bent on completing his pitiless work." But miraculously, no lives were lost and most of the guests were able to save their personal belongings.

In a eulogy, the newspaper offered this comment: "We trust that a new Jefferson will rise from the ashes of the old. But should it not, let our people rest assured that Richmond will not long be without another grand hotel somewhere. We are forging ahead in all directions too rapidly for that not to be the case." But there was hope. The 110 rooms that had escaped the fire were reopened, and the rebuilt Jefferson was designed to be fire resistant. It remained Richmond's best-known hotel and the place where the rich and famous gathered. It was the place to see and be seen.

But on March 10, 1944, it happened again. A fire broke out at a time when the hotel was filled with guests, many of whom were members of the Virginia General Assembly, which was in session.

Apparently, this fire started in a linen closet on the second-floor landing in the east wing. Possibly someone had carelessly discarded a cigarette or there was a spontaneous combustion. From the second floor, the fire extended to the fourth, fifth and sixth floors. A porter confirmed this when he said, "The fire apparently started in a stairway near the linen closet on the second floor. In a violent rush of flame and smoke, the fire ripped upwards. The major fire seemed to have skipped the second and third floors. When it reached the fifth and sixth floors, it burst down the hallway of the east wing, scorching the walls, covering the rooms with dense smoke, and trapping the guests in their rooms."

Firefighters from Engine 9 responded from their quarters at 801 North Fifth Street. They were soon joined by eight other engine companies, three truck companies, the reserve wagon and the foam wagon. The units laid 7,700 feet of hose to fight the fire. The newspaper reported, "Shortly after the fire broke out, women were screaming for help from the upper windows. All floors above the fourth floor were reported to be filled with smoke and that it was almost impossible for anyone except firefighters to traverse the halls."

There was much confusion as firefighters broke into upper-floor windows to rescue trapped people with ladders, and scantily clad guests who could do so rushed down the halls and stairways. Others who were trapped lowered themselves from windows with sheets tied together while firefighters carried people to safety. The firefighters were true heroes.

In room 501, Delegate Delameter Davis of Norfolk and his wife noticed a funny smell. They then realized the hotel was on fire. The delegate said, "I went to the window and, my God, the flames were creeping up by our window. I opened the door and smoke and flames hit me in the face. I slammed it shut and yelled to my wife to get in the bathroom. We got in there, turned on the light, and closed the door." The delegate and his wife used wet towels to survive by covering their faces. Soon, a British sailor and an American soldier broke into their room and helped them escape the flames. In room 595, Senator and Mrs. Garland Gray fled down the fire escape when they smelled smoke, but all of their personal property was destroyed. Senator and Mrs. S.F. Landreth, in room 602, used wet sheets to cover the doors and stayed in the bathroom until they were rescued. Firefighters commented that they had never seen such thick smoke. One firefighter was injured when he fell through the burning floor. He survived.

Room 600, on the sixth floor, was occupied by Mrs. James Hubert Price, widow of the former governor of Virginia, James Hubert Price. Mrs. Price, the former Lillian M. Martin, served as the state's first lady from 1938 to 1942 and was remembered as a very gracious lady. She died in the fire. The newspaper reported, "Seldom had Richmond had a more poignant tragedy than that which took the life of the gentle, gracious, and high-minded widow of Governor Price." She was identified by the wedding ring she still wore on her finger.

Also brought down from the sixth floor was Senator Aubrey G. Weaver of Front Royal, Virginia, who was referred to as the "Kingfish of the Senate." He was a leader in Virginia politics; and if someone wanted to know something about state government, he or she asked Senator Weaver. His wife was giving birth to a child and was not in the hotel. The senator was pronounced dead in the lobby. When Dr. J. Fulmer Bright saw the senator on the floor, he exclaimed, "My God, that's Senator Weaver and I think he is done for!" Two women were found suffocated in a bathroom where they had gone to avoid the advancing, raging fire. All of those who died were on the fifth and sixth floors.

A truly heroic rescue took place when an eighty-five-foot fire department ladder was raised by the fire department to the fifth floor, but it would not reach the sixth floor. The firemen used a pamper ladder, which is a type of ladder that can be attached to a windowsill by a hook on the end of the ladder. The firefighters would stand on the last rung of the aerial ladder and use the hook on the pamper ladder to crash through and hook onto an upper window. The firefighter would then climb up to the window and stand in the windowsill and repeat the process until the desired floor was reached. With the ladder up against the wall of the building, the firefighter could climb up the side of a building to rescue people who were beyond the reach of aerial ladders. Three firefighters using this dangerous piece of equipment managed to save a man from jumping by bringing him down the ladder. One of the firefighters involved in the rescue was E.A. Sherry, who eventually became chief of the Richmond Fire Department.

Every available ambulance in the city was dispatched to the Jefferson. Twelve people were taken to the Medical College of Virginia Hospital, and at least one man walked to nearby Grace Hospital to get treatment. Many local physicians were on scene to render aid, and Father Robert E. O'Kane of St. Paul's Catholic Church was there to administer the last rites and provide comfort to the injured.

Some people took advantage of the fire by going into the hotel and stealing money, clothing, jewelry and other items of value from the recently vacated rooms. Before the fire cooled, one man was sentenced to six months in jail for stealing an alarm clock and a purse containing $6.50. Justice was quick, and there was much condemnation of such larceny in the newspapers.

Following the fire, the Jefferson Hotel was criticized for not being prepared for the fire. Deficiencies included the following: the hose in the hotel was

Jefferson Hotel in 2015. *Photograph by Walter S. Griggs Jr.*

rotten, the fire extinguishers did not work, water pressure was too low and the fire department's hoses would not connect to the stand pipes in the hotel. These deficiencies led to numerous lawsuits against the Jefferson.

Although six people died and many were injured, the damage to the hotel was not extensive. Indeed, the Saturday night dance given by the Junior League of Richmond for soldiers was held on schedule. In the years ahead, the Jefferson would suffer through good times and bad times, but today, it is once again the place to see and be seen in Richmond. If the wandering spirit of Lewis Ginter visited the Jefferson Hotel today, he would be very proud of his creation.

## Chapter 10

# STOP, LOOK, LISTEN AND WATCH OUT FOR FALLING TRAINS

## 1903, 1912 AND 1960

These railroad stories are about disasters that could have happened but amazingly did not occur. But they do remind us to look out for falling trains when we eat in Shockoe Bottom restaurants and to be careful at railroad crossings because the locomotive might not have an engineer.

I love to eat pizza at a restaurant in Shockoe Slip. The slip is filled with restaurants, clubs and nightspots that are located under a maze of railroad bridges, crossings and viaducts. You can hardly finish a pizza without seeing or hearing the rumble and roar from a train passing overhead on the Chesapeake and Ohio (now CSX) viaduct.

In the late 1890s, the Chesapeake and Ohio Railroad began construction on a very high viaduct that would run parallel to the James River from the Lee Bridge to the Fulton Railroad Yards. Unlike most viaducts, this three-mile-long viaduct ran parallel to the James River but did not cross it. The first train passed over the viaduct on June 24, 1901.

The completion of the viaduct also created Richmond's famous three-level main line railroad crossing with the Southern Railway on the ground level, a second viaduct operated by the Seaboard Airline Railway passed over the Southern tracks and the new Chesapeake and Ohio viaduct crossed over the other two. This crossing became a tourist attraction and was featured on many different postcards. Indeed, Shockoe Bottom was filled with trains. Today, you do not have to wait long to see trains coming down the viaduct heading west to Westham or east to the Fulton Yards.

This maze of tracks passes over many buildings, parking lots, streets and my pizza place. I have often stopped eating my pizza to watch a train pass overhead. I have wondered if there was a chance that a train might fall off of the viaduct and land on my pizza. After thinking about this possibility, I did some research and discovered that trains have fallen off of the CSX viaduct into buildings and onto streets but not onto pizzas.

In July 1903, a train pulling boxcars loaded with barrels of cement departed Fulton Yards. Suddenly, a boxcar "jumped the rails, and after bumping along the rails for some distance, it plunged off the high steel viaduct and crashed into the rear of two stores: The Union Clothing Company and Joseph Johnson's Shoes and Trunk Store both on East Main Street," reported the *Richmond Times-Dispatch*. The owner of the clothing store did not realize that there had been an accident since he had become so used to the noise of trains going over his store. He only realized it when he saw people running into the street. Cement barrels broke through the boxcar and landed in the street. The cement, mixed with water, turned the street white. A reporter commented that the cement had been "scattered in picturesque confusion." Fortunately, no one was injured when the boxcar took flight.

The *Richmond Times-Dispatch* reported the incident:

> *A freight train was coming from Fulton. One of the cars, presumably the one which went to swift destruction, got off the track. It is said the brakeman signaled frantically towards the engine, forward, but the men in the locomotive, looking at the track before them, bowled along at a neat clip, blissfully unconscious of what was going on in the rear...The crippled [car] quit the game and made that fatal leap into the south end of the Main Street stores.*

Two other cars were derailed but did not leave the viaduct. Thousands of people gathered to see the wreck and destruction. In one of the buildings, a couple was eating dinner. They were not hurt but considered it "a rude interruption at an unexpected moment." What could have turned out to be a disaster became more of a public spectacle.

It happened again in 1912. A train of empty freight cars was headed to the Fulton Yards over the viaduct. The train derailed at Fourteenth and Dock Streets, and two empty gondolas "were hurled off [with] one crashing partly through the roof of the Southern Railway Freight Warehouse. The second car swung over the side of the viaduct without reaching the ground, while a third was turned over on the tracks. Two blocks back a freight car on the same train telescoped and stood up on its head." Fortunately, once again, no one was hurt, but it was a close call. The newspaper reported, "Directly under the gondola which was thrown headforemost first, a wagon loaded with hay was just ready to pull out. The horses plunged wildly from fright, but workers unhitched and removed them at great personal risk. Had the cars been loaded with coal, there would have been serious loss of life." The probable cause of the wreck was that the front wheels of an empty car had jumped the track. It was remarkable that no one was injured or killed. The main concerns were the frightened horses.

It has been a long time since a major accident has caused railroad cars to leave the viaduct and crash into buildings, but it could happen again. It is possible that one evening while listening to a train go over a restaurant, I will hear something unusual and find a boxcar, or perhaps a locomotive, in my pizza.

The other strange event occurred in 1960, when Atlantic Coast Line locomotive 240 left the freight yard in Richmond and headed west on the Chesapeake and Ohio tracks. What was unusual about this was the fact that the locomotive did not have an engineer. It was a runaway locomotive

A CSX train going over Shockoe Bottom. *Photograph by Walter S. Griggs Jr.*

headed to western Virginia. It sped through multiple railroad crossings without blowing a whistle. Remarkably, there were no accidents. A C&O engineer took a locomotive out on a parallel track and reached into the cab of the ACL engine with a "packing hook, tapped the independent brake, and slowed the engine." Then he boarded the ACL locomotive and stopped it in Fluvanna County.

An ACL yard worker quipped, "No. 240's assignment in the yard was not a particularly exciting one." The *Richmond Times-Dispatch* began its story with this sentence: "Locomotive No. 240, its unscheduled joyride into western Virginia over, came home yesterday to resume its drab life of shifting railroad cars in the Atlantic Coast Line yard." But it could not have started on that trip alone. Railroad men were convinced that the locomotive was started by a disgruntled employee, and it was absolutely amazing that the runaway locomotive did not hit another train or a car at a crossing.

Some disasters in life can be avoided, but the risks of workin' on the railroad are very real and could put your pizza in jeopardy. Sometimes a disaster is averted by the slightest thing, and if something had gone a different way, a tragedy would have occurred.

## Chapter 11

# FIRE ON THE JAMES

## 1904

Because the James River flows through Richmond, Richmond is known as the "River City." The Native Americans were the first to sail on the James in their canoes. Then in 1607, the English arrived, and Captain Christopher Newport and his followers sailed up the James and placed a cross on what would one day be the site of the city of Richmond. Since the arrival of the English and the establishment of the city, the James River has been very important to Richmonders as a beautiful river, a scenic venue, a place to watch birds and a place for recreation. People also flock to the river for kayaking, swimming, hiking and fishing.

But at one time, the river was used by steamboats that would travel up and down between Richmond and Norfolk. One of these steamboats was named after the Indian maiden who saved Captain John Smith from death at Jamestown: Pocahontas. She was described by one writer as a "woman who in beauty of mind and charm of person was in every way a princess."

The *Pocahontas* was constructed in 1893 by the Harlan and Hollingsworth Company of Wilmington, Delaware, and was launched in the Delaware River. Shortly thereafter, it became the property of the Virginia Navigation Company and was commanded by Captain C.C. Graves. A brochure described the *Pocahontas*:

> *The palace Steamer* Pocahontas—*No steam vessel so entirely suited to first class travel in points of elegance, speed, safety, and comfort in all weather, as the* Pocahontas, *has ever before been seen in southern waters.*

*Upon the main deck…were the social hall and separate parlor saloons for lady passengers and servants respectively…The large dining room below is furnished in exquisite taste, and the menu equaled in quality and variety as that of the best hotels.*

*The central feature of the steamer was the large and costly electric orchestrion upon which the choicest selections of popular compositions are performed during the trip with the excellence and effect of a band of thirty pieces. The motive machinery of the steamer was of the highest class, and it is heated throughout with steam and lighted by electricity.*

The steamer's dimensions were 203 feet long, its weight was 814 gross tons and there was a crew of twenty-seven. It was propelled through the water by two large paddle wheels mounted on each side of the steamboat.

Once the *Pocahontas* entered service, the steamboat was a familiar sight on the James River. Every Monday, Wednesday and Friday, it left Richmond at 7:00 a.m. and arrived in Norfolk the same day at 5:30 p.m. The fare was $1.50 for one way and $2.50 for a round trip. Between Richmond and Norfolk, it stopped at City Point, Claremont, Jamestown, Scotland, Hog Island, Fergusson, Newport News and Old Point Comfort. On the way, passengers could see many historical places along the James River or they could play cards, smoke, listen to music or relax on the hurricane deck. In addition to these trips, the steamer made frequent moonlight excursions carrying various church groups and other organizations. The *Pocahontas* was successful and very popular with Richmonders.

But then disaster occurred. On April 30, 1904, the *Pocahontas* had arrived at its dock at Rockets below Richmond and had unloaded the cargo. A fire was discovered on board the steamboat. Most of the crew had gone home, but there were some narrow escapes. One man was reported "blinded and crazed by smoke and fell overboard." Another man jumped overboard and was saved from drowning. The engineer and his wife were on board. They escaped, but the wife did not have time to put on her shoes.

Fire alarms were turned in from fire alarm boxes at Main and Nicholson Streets and Main and Ash Streets. When first discovered, the fire was no larger than a man's hat. The fire department responded, as did two tugboats—the *Thomas Cunningham Sr.* and the *E.V. McCaully*. Water was poured on the burning steamboat from land and sea, but it continued to burn out of control. The flames accelerated and attracted over one thousand people to Libby Hill Park to observe the fire. Eventually, the weight of the water being poured on to the boat caused it to sink into the James River mud. It was reported, "The destruction of this beautiful steamer is well-nigh total, to all outward appearances. But the hull below the water line is of steel and of course uninjured."

By 11:00 p.m., the fire had burned itself out. "The saloon and deck works were charred and twisted ruins, in pathetic and striking contrast to the life and light and beauty in which the steamer has so many times been seen on moonlight excursions and other festive occasions." Another writer said, "The *Pocahontas*, which had so proudly and swiftly plied the historic water of Virginia's chief river, was burned to the water's edge and sunk." The "Princess of the James" was buried in the mud of the James River.

There were several theories about where the fire started. Some thought it started in the engine room, others thought the fire started in the kitchen or in some electrical wiring. The actual cause was never determined, but the *Pocahontas* would sail again. Divers found that its steel hull was still sound, as was the engine. The *Pocahontas* was pumped out and towed down the James River, up the Chesapeake Bay, through the Delaware and Chesapeake canal to Roach's Shipyard at Chester, Pennsylvania, where it was rebuilt using the original plans.

Returning to service, the *Pocahontas* continued to sail the James until 1939, when it was sold for scrap. But the steamer was certainly a credit to its namesake and provided lasting memories for all who sailed on it. The beauty of a steamboat sailing down the James River on a moonlit night with the lights reflecting on the calm waters was a sight whose beauty truly honored the lovely Indian maiden, Pocahontas.

## Chapter 12

# THE SPANISH FLU EPIDEMIC

## 1918 AND 1919

My first memory of being sick was the day a nurse took a cork with a needle sticking out of it from a test tube filled with alcohol and stuck my finger with the needle to get some blood. She then wiped the needle off and stuck it back into the test tube filled with alcohol. I suspect it was used and reused until the cork wore out or the needle got dull. At that point in my life, I knew nothing about the great flu epidemic that had virtually paralyzed Richmond; I only knew that my finger hurt.

Later, I learned about the flu epidemic of 1918–19 when my grandfather told me that he had had the flu in 1918 but recovered from it. He seemed to take great pride in recovering from the flu, which he described as a miserable experience that caused him to float between life and death. He always believed that his deep religious faith saved his life; and for the rest of his life, he wore a small gold cross on his suit coat.

No one is quite certain where the influenza epidemic of 1918–19 began. It acquired the name Spanish flu because it was widely reported in the Spanish newspaper that the Spanish royal family had the flu. It was also called by a number of other names, including la grippe, the flu, grippe and the Spanish influenza. Before it abated, it would kill more people than any other disease in human history, including the infamous Black Death of the Middle Ages.

Most historians trace the origin of the flu in the United States to Camp Funston, Kansas. In the last week of February 1918, the soldiers began to get sick. As the soldiers moved from camp to camp and around the world fighting World War I, they carried the flu with them. Eventually, the flu infected Camp Lee near Petersburg, Virginia, which was very close to Richmond. The flu first appeared in Camp Lee on September 13, 1918, but no one seemed to know anything about it. By September 17, there were over five hundred cases at Camp Lee. A few days later, there were over ten thousand cases. Obviously, the physicians now knew they were dealing with an epidemic. In response, the camp was closed to visitors, and there were no public gatherings permitted. However, training was continued because soldiers were needed for World War I. Unfortunately, some soldiers continued to train before they were well, which resulted in relapse or even death. Camp Lee was virtually paralyzed by the flu, which overwhelmed the medical staff and the facilities.

It was obvious that the illness that had shut down Camp Lee would eventually spread to Richmond because the two cities were so close to each other, and soldiers frequently traveled to Richmond for dances and entertainment. Richmond's city health officers tried to find a way to deal with the inevitable threat to the city. They determined the best approach was a public education campaign to advise Richmonders about the flu. Some advice was in poetic form. For example, there was this widely published public health poem:

*If you'd dodge the Spanish "flu,"*
*Do not sneeze and do not chew*
*Any gum in public places.*
*Then the microbes won't get you*
*If you wheeze the weird cadenza of Castilian influenza,*
*But the doctors can't tell whenza.*

In spite of the best efforts at education, by the end of September, the flu had spread to Richmond with several hundred reported cases.

One can only imagine what it must have been like to know that you were getting the flu and that there was no real cure. A person who contracted the flu had a number of symptoms, including a temperature over 102 degrees, a sore throat, exhaustion, headaches, pain in the limbs, bloodshot eyes, a cough, sometimes a nose bleed and, in some cases, would turn blue. Since these symptoms could also replicate other illnesses, it was sometimes difficult to diagnosis the flu; sometimes the patient would seem to get well and then relapse. Many healthy young adults succumbed to the flu, which was unusual since the elderly were usually the ones to die from it.

If you caught the flu, the treatment usually consisted of patent medications that could be found in the drugstore, including Vicks VapoRub. One woman recommended Earl's Hypo-Cod, which "chased away the troubles with the flu." Pe-Ru-Na was also recommended since "it stands off lots of doctor bills and makes you feel like a new person." Another product was Foley's Honey and Tar, which "puts a soothing, healing coating on the rough, inflamed throat, clears the mucus, stops the coughing and dry tickling, and ceases the tightness and hard breathing." There was a toothpaste called Kolynoe Dental Cream that was supposed to stop the flu virus from getting into you. To remove poison from the system, Dr. Pierce's Pleasant Pellets were recommended. One Richmond doctor "soaked the legs and feet of flu patients in scalding water, and then swaddled the patient in blankets until they were red and sweating." These medications and treatments may or may not have had any value. Unfortunately, there was no vaccine to prevent the flu, which continued to spread.

The *Richmond Times-Dispatch* on October 1, 1918, reported that 425 cases of the flu had been diagnosed in Richmond, with 18 cases at Westhampton College of the University of Richmond. *The Collegian*, the student newspaper, reported that the girls had "bought out the corner drugstore" but still got the flu. One hallway in North Court was converted into a ward for flu patients. Fortunately, all of the students recovered.

It was believed that the disease had not spread as rapidly in Richmond because of public education programs about the flu and because Richmonders had "taken precautions against catching the disease."

But people continued to get the flu in spite of the educational programs and other efforts. It was reported that trying "to stop the flu was like trying to stop a cold. Influenza was disseminated by coughing, sneezing in people's faces, drinking out of common drinking cups, putting fingers in the mouth, and by all the ways in which saliva was transmitted." The onset of the disease was so rapid that people would fall off of their horses or just fall down. In some cases, a person would die within twelve hours from the onset of the illness.

Public health officials warned against being in crowds, such as at the movies, soda fountains, restaurants or church. It was also believed that proper ventilation would help prevent the disease, so places of public assembly had to be properly ventilated. Also, brochures were distributed providing the following advice:

*Avoid needless crowding.*
*Smother your coughs and sneezes.*
*Your nose, not your mouth, was made to breathe thru.*
*Remember the 3 C's, clean mouth, clean skin, and clean clothes.*
*Food will win the war....Help by choosing and chewing your food well.*
*Wash your hands before eating.*
*Avoid tight clothes, tight shoes, tight gloves—seek to make nature your ally,*
    *not your prisoner.*
*When the air is pure, breathe all of it you can—breathe deeply.*

But in spite of these efforts, the flu continued to make Richmonders sick. It was not long before poems about the flu began to appear in the newspaper. One such poem is as follows:

*O, Flu:*
*When you get up in the morning with a chill*
*With a chill*
*And you realize a slacking in your will*
*When you sneeze.*
*When you wheeze.*
*When you tremble in the knees,*
*Grab the telephone and order in a doctor and a pill.*

*For you've got it—got the Flu:*
*And I don't mind telling you*
*That it's not a little nice to be a victim of the Flu*
*And you'll know it when you get the Spanish Flu.*
*It's the grippe and influenza at their best.*
*Very best.*
*And the health departments label it a pest.*
*It's a bear.*
*And they swear*
*When it tackles you for fair*
*It's a very undesirable sort of uninvited guest.*

*It annoys you, does the Flu.*
*As indispositions go*
*When equipped to make a blooming red-nosed jackass out of you.*
*Which is why I do not like the Spanish Flu,*

*When you ask the doctor how to flop the flu*
*Flop the flu*
*He will pass a lot of good advice to you.*
*But the nice*
*Kind advice*
*Doesn't really cut much ice,*
*For you'll get it if you get it and in spite of what you do.*
*So perdition to the Flu!*
*When your nose starts turning blue*
*And you sneeze and wheeze and shiver till you don't know what to do.*
*You can bet you're entertaining Spanish flu.*

In early October, it was reported that there were 849 cases of the flu in Richmond, but public health officials told Richmonders that it was not a fatal disease, although people were dying. Medical professionals advised, "When the symptoms begin to appear take a dose of oil or another mild purgative. Then indulge in a good hot bath and wrap up in bed with about five grains of quinine inside of you. Sweat the grippe out and stay in bed at least 48 hours. If the head aches severely, take aspirin, or better yet, apply cold towels to the head."

And there was this poem:

*Obey the laws,*
*And wear the gauze,*
*Protect yourself,*
*From septic paws.*

Soon, the newspaper reported that some people had died of the flu with over one thousand reported cases in the city. The next day, there were two thousand cases, and the situation was considered grave. Attendance at public gatherings was down, but public schools stayed open. Although a lot of advice was being given, the truth was that there was no cure for the flu.

Then, on October 6, drastic action was taken. Schools, churches and theaters were ordered closed by the city health officer. Churches were urged not to use the common cup for communion services. Some churches, including St. John's Church at Stuart Circle, opted for outdoor services, and all pleasure trips to Camp Lee were forbidden. In addition, efforts were launched to recruit nurses. In a break with Jim Crowism, race did not matter if you were a nurse.

By October 10, there were ten thousand reported cases of the flu in Richmond. John Marshall High School was converted into an emergency hospital for white patients. Bellevue School held the overflow from John Marshall, and Baker School was the emergency hospital for African Americans. It was sometimes difficult to get to the hospital since streetcar operators were also ill with the flu and could not work. In spite of the difficulties, the ladies of Second Presbyterian Church and many other churches made soup for those with the flu. The ladies at Second Presbyterian asked the congregation to bring pint and quart jars to church to be filled with soup.

A nurse wrote about the flu:

*This pesky flu is all over town! And white and black and rich and poor are all included in its tour. I had to nurse two victims of this latest curse. Thank heaven! They are slightly better. Believe you me, they kept me busy. I've turned about till I am dizzy. The picture shows are closed up tight, the soda fountains have the blight, and everybody stays at home (safety first—afraid to roam.)*

And the following appeared in the society column:

*On account of the epidemic of Spanish grippe, invitations have been recalled for the marriage of Miss Nellie Scott Payne to Lieutenant Edward Nelson Smith, United States Army. The wedding, which was to have taken place Saturday evening at 6 o'clock in the First Presbyterian Church, will now be celebrated on the same date but very quietly at the apartment of the bride's aunt, Miss Hattie L. Scott, in Westchester. Only the immediate families will witness the ceremony.*

There were many other similar notices in the paper.

There were also many notices of meetings being called off because of the flu. For example, the Baptist Woman's Missionary Union meeting was called off. At the same time, the Richmond chapter of the United Daughters of the Confederacy postponed its meeting, as did most of the other organizations in the area.

Taking up even more space in the newspaper were the obituaries of those who had died from the Spanish flu and pneumonia. The obituary of Robert E. Rice was poignant. It stated, "Mr. Rice sacrificed his life in the performance of his duty, having stuck to his post filling prescriptions for

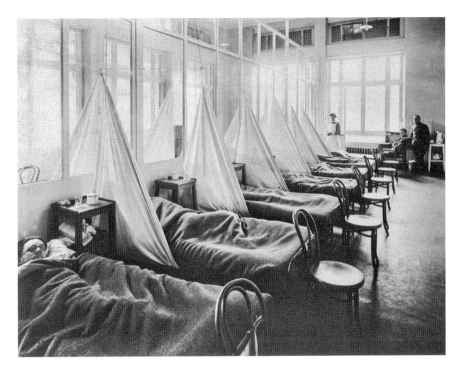

Spanish flu patients. *Courtesy of Wikimedia Commons.*

influenza patients when he was ill with the disease from which he died." He was thirty-three years old.

By mid-October, the situation seemed to be well in hand. Milk was thought to be helpful, and preference was given to babies and sick people in its distribution. Children would skip rope while repeating:

> *I had a little bird.*
> *Its name was Enza.*
> *I opened the window.*
> *And in-flu-enza.*

Although the flu situation was reported to be under control, it was still making people sick in the city. Each day, the papers reported more cases and printed more obituaries. There were furious efforts to find a way to cure the flu. Dr. George Baer suggested an injection of a "sterile solution representing 1.54 grams of iodine in chemical combination with creosote and guarcol." Another cure was to "go to bed and stay quiet—take a laxative—eat plenty of Nourishing food—keep up your strength. Nature is the cure." It was also suggested that you call a doctor. By October 14, there were over fourteen thousand cases in Richmond with six deaths reported. But the newspapers seemed to switch between optimism and pessimism. Some reports indicated that the flu was dissipating, only to be followed by reports that it was on the increase. The illness seemed to come in waves.

To deal with the epidemic, Richmond was divided into four districts with doctors and nurses assigned to each sector. To meet the needs of the sick, there were constant requests for nurses—or, for that matter, anyone who had any medical training. One advertisement offered nurses the pay of forty dollars a week, and trained attendants were paid twenty-five dollars per week. They were asked to report to the John Marshall High School at the Marshall Street entrance.

Amid the tragic situation, the newspaper started to publish more poems about the flu, including this sad one:

> *Come, kiss me, dear…just touch your lips*
> *To mine, so I may know*
> *The Angel of my Shadow Days*
> *Regrets to see me go.*
> *It's only that you've been so kind,*
> *So good;…The bugles…Hear…*
> *Quick, I must go;…They need me;…come!*
> *O, God,…Come kiss me, dear!*

By late October, based on a Boy Scout survey, it was reported that the situation might be getting better. By the first of November, the newspapers reported that the epidemic seemed to be abating.

On November 5, 1918, restrictions on public gatherings were lifted. The city faced a lot of pressure from theater owners who had lost a considerable amount of money due to the closings. However, people were still getting sick and dying. Over six hundred people had died by early November. There were so many deaths in Richmond that coffins were stacked on top of one another at Main Street Station waiting for transportation. In some communities, there was a shortage of undertakers, and dead bodies had to be kept in the homes where the persons died. It was a gruesome sight.

On November 11, 1918, World War I ended, giving a measure of peace to a war-torn world. Richmonders celebrated the end of the conflict, and the city went wild with joy. Broad Street was filled with people screaming and yelling while church bells were ringing, but the war on the flu continued. The *Richmond Times-Dispatch* noted that more Americans died from the Spanish flu in the "last four months than America's losses by death in the nineteen months of war."

After Christmas 1918, the epidemic abated but continued into the summer, when it finally left the state. But the damage had been done. Almost 21,000 Richmonders had had the flu, and almost 1,000 people had died from it. Worldwide it had killed more than 100 million people. There are no memorials in Richmond to those who died in the epidemic, but there are a lot of tombstones with the death date 1918 or 1919 chiseled into them.

# Chapter 13
# THE COLLAPSE OF THE CHURCH HILL TUNNEL

## 1925

*Oft, when I feel my engine swerve,*
*As o'er strange rails we fare,*
*I strain my eyes around the curve*
*For what awaits us there.*
*When swift and free she carries me*
*Through yards unknown at night,*
*I look along the line to see*
*That all the lamps are white.*

*The blue light marks the crippled car,*
*The green light signals slow,*
*The red light is a danger light,*
*The white light, "Let her go."*
*Again the open fields we roam,*
*And when the night is fair,*
*I look up in the starry dome*
*And wonder what's up there.*

*For who can speak for those who dwell*
*Behind the curving sky?*
*No man has ever lived to tell*
*Just what it means to die.*
*Swift toward life's terminal I tread*
*The run seems short tonight.*
*God only knows what's at the end—*
*I hope the lamps are white.*
*—Cy Warman*

**M**y grandfather ran a grocery store on Twenty-fifth Street in Church Hill in 1945. In an old orange truck, he made deliveries to his customers. Late one afternoon when rain was falling, he drove me down an old dirt road and pointed out a sealed-up tunnel. He said, "There are dead men and a train in that tunnel." From that moment to this, I have been fascinated by the Church Hill Tunnel. The tunnel was built during the glory days of railroading when powerful steam locomotives ruled the rails and carried freight and passengers across the continent. Unfortunately, there were frequent wrecks, and some of them have been immortalized in song. The death of Casey Jones, who was trying to make up time, is still remembered as a "trip to the promised land." The wreck that happened outside Danville, Virginia, is still recalled in a song, "Wreck of the Old '97," because the train was "going downhill making 90 miles per hour when the whistle broke into a scream." The engineer was found "scalded to death by the steam."

Although the Church Hill Tunnel story has never rivaled the death of Casey Jones or the wreck of Old '97 in popularity, it is an interesting part of Richmond's history, and everyone seems to know something about the collapse of the tunnel. It is a railroad story that has always fascinated Richmonders.

The story began on February 1, 1872, when construction started on the Church Hill Tunnel. The tunnel was designed to connect the Chesapeake and Ohio Railroad tracks in Shockoe Valley at Seventeenth Street with the docks on the James River at Rockets Landing. Although there were experts who felt that it was a mistake to construct a tunnel through the unstable ground under Church Hill, the engineers and the C&O felt that the tunnel was feasible. In digging the tunnel, the engineers prevailed over the geologists.

During the course of construction, there were numerous cave-ins resulting in several deaths and many serious injuries, but the work continued. The tunnel was finally completed, and on December 11, 1873, a locomotive named the David Anderson steamed through it. One of the longest tunnels in the United States was now in service. Unfortunately, the shallow James River prevented large oceangoing vessels from coming to Richmond, and the city of Richmond did not deepen the channel in the river as it had promised. With the Port of Richmond inadequate, the C&O extended its tracks to reach the deep-water port at Newport News, Virginia. When the new route was completed, the Church Hill Tunnel was used less and less frequently.

Richmonders, who were frustrated that the James River had proven to be inadequate for river commerce, commented that they could always sit

The sealed-up western entrance to the Church Hill Tunnel. *Photograph by Walter S. Griggs Jr.*

on a bench in Chimborazo Park and watch the trains go to Newport News. In 1902, the last scheduled train passed through the tunnel. It was found unsafe for further use in 1915, and for the next ten years, it remained closed. However, by 1925, rail traffic had increased, and the C&O began repairing the tunnel so that it could be returned to service and relieve the traffic on other lines.

As work was progressing in the tunnel, disaster struck. Around 3:00 p.m. on October 2, 1925, engineer Tom Mason kissed his wife, left his home and walked to the corner of the block. For some reason, he turned around, went back to his house and kissed his wife again. He, along with his fireman, Ben Mosby, then headed to Fulton Yards and climbed aboard locomotive No. 231. Mason then released the brake, opened the throttle and began to pull a string of ten flatcars into the Church Hill Tunnel so that the laborers could load them with dirt. The train was under Twentieth Street beneath Jefferson Park when a few bricks in the tunnel's roof fell with a splash into the pools of water on the tunnel floor. The falling bricks caused the electrical connections to break, and the tunnel was thrown into darkness. Carpenters working at the eastern portal of the tunnel near Chimborazo Park, about a mile from the cave-in, felt a sharp swish of air, and they immediately ran into the rain

Locomotive 231 while in the service of the Chicago, Cincinnati and Louisville Railroad. *Photograph Courtesy of the Railway and Locomotive Historical Society.*

falling outside. As the workers were running out of the tunnel, 190 feet of the 4,000-foot tunnel collapsed under Jefferson Park.

Then Mosby yelled, "Watch out, Tom, she's coming in!" Seconds later, Mosby and Mason were scalded by steam escaping from the crushed locomotive. In spite of severe burns, Mosby slipped out of the locomotive's cab, crawled under the flatcars behind the locomotive and escaped from the collapsing tunnel. When he emerged at the eastern end, he told bystanders to tell his wife and little girl that he was all right. He died the next day in Grace Hospital.

Engineer Mason was a large man and, unlike Mosby, could not slide out of the locomotive's cab. R.C. Gary, a foreman, was at work on the eastern end of the tunnel when he felt the sharp swish of air as the mass of dirt fell in. Running to the locomotive, he made a desperate effort to get Mason out, but the engineer was pinned by debris and by the reverse lever that was lodged firmly across his chest. A.S. Adams, the flagman on the doomed train, was standing on a flatcar when the first bricks began to fall. He was able to dive under the car and crawl out of the tunnel. Charles Kelso was also in the tunnel when it collapsed and escaped by crawling to safety using the flatcars as an escape tunnel within the collapsed tunnel. Cut on the head, he was sent home in a cab by C&O. He never talked about his close encounter with death. Harold Glen and his father, John B. Glenn, were both working in the tunnel at the time of the cave-in. Fortunately, they heard the noise of the collapsing tunnel and were able to escape. Harold Glenn immediately called his girlfriend, Annie L. Walter, to let her know that he was not hurt.

Crumbling clay, collapsing supports, falling bricks, splitting wood, screaming men and escaping steam from the dying locomotive echoed throughout the collapsed, dark, damp, muddy tunnel. Survivors recalled the eerie screams of the terror-filled men rushing though the blackness to either safety or death. A carpenter gave the following account of the disaster:

> *Men approached me screaming and fighting. Some of them yelled that they had knives and would cut anybody who got in their way. The confusion lasted for a long time it seems. There were no lights. Men ran back and forth bewildered. Some of them ran toward the cave-in. Others butted their heads into the sidewalls, fell over the ties and rails and knocked each other down. We did not know what had happened or what was going to happen.*

At the cave-in site, rumors were rampant. There were many reports of people hearing noises inside the tunnel. Richmonders kept up hope that Mason and the others trapped might still be alive. The *Richmond Times-Dispatch* reported, "Tom Mason might be at his throttle, his burned body supported by the loose clay which had poured in under the roof of the locomotive cab." Also missing were two African American laborers, Richard Lewis and H. Smith. But were there more laborers in the tunnel? One story emerged that the workers in the tunnel had been issued work boots that were to be returned to the roundhouse at the end of the day. Many of these boots were never returned. Were they on the feet of men trapped in the tunnel? It is also possible that some laborers came from the Deep South seeking jobs. They might have gone into the tunnel to find a foreman when the tunnel caved in on them. Perhaps they were never found and were not missed by their families since they were not expected to return to their homes. It will probably always be a mystery how many men came to their final resting place within the Church Hill Tunnel.

People flocked to the site of the cave-in. A favorite viewing site was the viaduct that connected Church Hill to downtown Richmond. Charles Williams remembered standing on the viaduct watching the rescue efforts with his father and two brothers. He recalled that the crowd was milling around waiting for news of the rescue effort. At a time of racial segregation in Richmond, blacks and whites stood together sharing a common hope and a fervent prayer that some men might still be found alive in the tunnel.

In an effort to rescue those who were trapped, a large steam shovel was used to cut into Jefferson Park. Unfortunately, the powerful steam shovel caused additional cave-ins and was taken out of service, and the C&O was forced to find another approach. Consequently, the railroad began digging shafts from the surface of Jefferson Park in an effort to reach the trapped train. This method seemed slow, and Richmonders were critical of the time it was taking to reach the train. To reduce public criticism, the C&O issued daily reports letting people know that every effort was being made to reach the train as quickly as possible.

Finally, on October 11, 1925, nine days after the cave-in, workers cut through a flatcar and crawled up to the locomotive. There they saw the body of the engineer. With the aid of an acetylene torch to cut through the reverse lever that pinned him to the seat, the dead engineer was freed. And at the top of the hill, Tom Mason's little boy, who had hoped and prayed that his daddy would be found alive, could now end his lonely vigil. Harold Glenn went back into the shaft from which Tom Mason had been removed and retrieved the engineer's lantern. He put the lantern down and continued to work. While he was working, someone took the lantern, and it was never returned.

Tom Mason's funeral was held at St. Patrick's Church, and Ben Mosby's was conducted at St. John's Church. Both of these churches were within a few yards of the tunnel that had claimed the lives of the two men.

For many days, the men of the C&O searched in vain for Richard Lewis and H. Smith and any other men who might have been buried in the tunnel, but no more bodies were found. Realizing that further searching would be futile, the C&O began to contemplate the future of the tunnel. Since only a small section had collapsed, it could have been repaired and put back into service. However, the tunnel had been a source of constant trouble and was not essential to the railroad's operation, so the C&O decided to fill it with sand. Because the removal of the locomotive and its cars would cost at least $30,000, far more than they were worth, railroad officials decided to bury them in the tunnel for all eternity. When the official decision to seal the train in the tunnel was made known, the *Richmond News Leader* said in the train's obituary, "The train might not be seen for another geological period when men of a new civilization discover a relic of the Twentieth Century in what once was the blue marl of Church Hill."

The eastern entrance to the Church Hill Tunnel in 1963. *Photograph by Walter S. Griggs Jr.*

Although the tunnel was closed, it has not been forgotten. There are still occasional cave-ins and persistent concerns on the part of those people whose property is on or near the tunnel. In 1955, the East End Post Office on Broad Street was "hurriedly abandoned because of cracks developing in its brick walls." There also were stories from time to time of houses reported to be sinking. And the eastern portal near Chimborazo Park has been used from time to time as a hideout for criminals and a place to deal drugs.

There are also strange stories of knocking sounds still coming from the tunnel and of men standing on a flatcar laughing as they passed the tunnel. The best-known urban legend is that a vampire runs down Main Street and enters the mausoleum of W.W. Poole in Hollywood Cemetery. Of course, these are just stories. Although it never became popular, Llewellyn Lewis, a brakeman on the Southern Railway, wrote the following poem in honor of his fellow railroaders who died in the tunnel:

*"The Train That Will Never Be Found"*

*Remember the Church Hill tunnel*
*Near a mile under Richmond town.*

Painting of a train leaving the Church Hill Tunnel. *Photograph by Walter S. Griggs Jr.*

*There's a story I want to tell you*
*Of a train that'll never be found.*

*On a bleak afternoon in the autumn*
*When the skies were overcast,*
*A train and its crew were working*
*In the tunnel performing their tasks.*

*No one dreamed of danger*
*Of a death that was hoverin' near*
*They were happy while they were working*
*For their loved ones home so dear.*

*When all of a sudden a tremble,*
*A large gap in the slimy clay*
*Then the earth claimed a few in its clutches,*
*In the darkness the rest groped their way.*

*Many shovels and picks were diggin'*
*For their pals in the buried train*
*But the cold slimy clay held its victims,*
*Soon their hopes were found in vain.*

*Many hours did they search for their comrades*
*Who might live in the cold, cold cave,*
*But they never found one who was living*
*Way down in that untimely grave.*

*Brothers, keep shovlin'*
*Pickin' in the ground.*
*Brothers, keep listenin'*
*For the train that's never been found.*

The train that has never been found and those who might still be buried with it in the Church Hill Tunnel are probably not recalled by the engineers who run the CSX trains within a few blocks of the tunnel. Yet I like to think that whenever a whistle blows on a locomotive, it is a tribute to Tom Mason, Ben Mosby, Richard Lewis, H. Smith and possibly other railroad men who joined that long line of men in blue overalls who were working on the railroad on that October day and took "their farewell trip to the promised land."

## Chapter 14

# DEATH IN THE MEHERRIN RIVER

## 1940

When a person or persons disappears and can not be found, it becomes a mystery. People want to find out what happened to them, especially if it is a loved one, a friend or a celebrity. Today, people still search for the Lost Colony, Amelia Earhart and all of the ships and planes that have disappeared in the Bermuda Triangle. There is one of these mysteries in my own family concerning the disappearance of Oscar Martin Feitig in November 1940.

Oscar Feitig was my second cousin. I saw him when I was two weeks old. I never saw him again. His subsequent disappearance has been a mystery that has haunted my family for years. A graduate of John Marshall High School, Oscar lived on King William Road in Richmond and was an operator in the distribution department of the Virginia Electric and Power Company. He had a bright future ahead of him.

Shortly after visiting my family, he and a friend named Lessie Deel, a graduate nurse from Johnston-Willis Hospital, drove to see Deel's sister in Lunenburg County, Virginia, on November 14, 1940. Following the visit, the couple headed back to Richmond on Route 667. According to Deel, they approached a temporary bridge called High Bridge over the Meherrin River that was built to replace one that had been washed away the previous summer. When they approached the bridge around 9:00 p.m., they "saw a large gap in the bridge but they could not stop in time." With breaks screaming, the automobile plunged fifty feet through the gap in the bridge into the muddy Meherrin River, which was about fifteen feet deep. The car had crashed through the temporary bridge, and the two people inside the sinking car struggled to survive.

When the vehicle hit the water, Deel was either pushed out of the car by Oscar Feitig or by the rush of the water. She did not know for sure. She lost consciousness and floated down the river before becoming aware of her surroundings. She grabbed some overhanging tree limbs, which she clung to for a long time, then pulled herself to shore and finally went to a house for help. The occupants of the farmhouse refused to help her, probably because she was wet and disheveled. She walked some more before reaching a second house. The occupant, William Daniel, immediately took her to South Hill, where she received medical treatment in a restaurant for exposure and cuts on her arms from a physician and a nurse who came to help her. Following medical treatment, the nurse drove her home to Richmond.

Immediately, a search was undertaken to find Oscar Feitig. Police chief B.L. Smithson of South Hill was committed to finding the body, and for the next several weeks, he did everything possible to find Oscar. To aid in finding him, a picture and a description were published in the local newspapers. It was reported that he was twenty-five years old, about six feet tall, weighed about 150 pounds and had dark hair and brown eyes. To find him, a massive search was launched, and over one thousand people visited the scene where the accident occurred. Although many were curiosity seekers, many were there to aid in the search.

Eventually, the car was located not far from the bridge, and it took three tries for a wrecker to pull it from the river. It was badly battered, with most of the glass broken, but Oscar was not in the car. There was no evidence there to indicate what happened to him.

On November 16, approximately one hundred persons were "working out of boats and from the shore; they were dragging the river and using grappling hooks in an effort to recover the body of Oscar Feitig," reported the *Richmond Times-Dispatch*. Since the river was swollen, the progress was slow and frustrating. Eventually, his overcoat was pulled out of the river with a grappling hook about a mile and a half from the bridge, but it was not initially known if he was wearing it or if it had floated out of the sunken automobile. Later, both Deel and her sister recalled that he had put on the overcoat before leaving for Richmond. The searchers also walked along the banks of the river on the theory that Oscar Feitig might have gotten to the bank of the river and then fallen back into the water and drowned. The search did not find any indication that he had reached the river's bank. By the third day of searching, people were sent to stand on bridges to look for the body in case it floated downstream.

The *Richmond Times-Dispatch* on November 19 reported that the searchers were using search lights provided by the Highway Department in an effort to work around the clock to locate the body. In a last desperate effort, Oscar Feitig's parents authorized the use of dynamite in an effort to bring the body to the surface of the river by an explosion. The effort was a failure.

The next attempt to find the body was to open a dam in order to lower the water level, but it did not yield any results. Wires were strung across the river to catch a floating body, but nothing was caught. The next approach was to carefully search the riverbank from the fallen bridge to Route 58, a distance of about eighteen miles. A search leader said, "The river has many holes and washed out places in which the body could have become lodged."

When their efforts failed, the request was made to have thirty men from the Civilian Conservation Corps (CCC) near Charlottesville aid in the search. Smithson felt that Oscar Feitig, like Lessie Deel, might have "reached the shore and collapsed somewhere near the bank of the river." He wanted to use the CCC to search the shore, houses and the inland area. Deel said Feitig had the coat on when he was driving. Since it was found in the river, it was believed he might have taken it off in an effort to swim to the shore. If he could take it off, it meant he was alive.

The request to use the CCC was denied because the corps could be used only when lives could be saved. The next step was to dig into the sandy banks from a raft, but this failed to yield any results. A month later, Oscar Feitig's father expressed the hope that his son might still be alive. Eventually, the search ended, and the body was never found, but every effort had been made to locate the body and provide some closure to the family who had lost their only child. It can truly be said that Smithson did everything possible to find Oscar Feitig.

As is generally the case, explanations were provided for why the bridge collapsed. Highway commissioner Henry G. Shirley asserted, "The temporary bridge, which was built after the original bridge was destroyed by the summer floods, was safe. The bridge had been built to carry traffic from South Hill and Kenbridge and could carry the weight of the vehicles that used it. But it was believed that debris floating in the river weakened the pilings that supported the bridge causing it to collapse with the weight of the car." Although there were no reports that high water had damaged other structures, the highway department was careful not to suggest that the temporary bridge was of poor construction or that the highway department was at fault. Mr. Shirley concluded, "It was an unfortunate accident but one of those things that could not be helped."

Family members offered several theories of what might have happened. My grandfather, Martin Feitig, believed Oscar Feitig went to a farmhouse, and, being wet and probably injured, was taken for some sort of criminal. He was then murdered and buried in an unmarked grave. Another theory was that he had lost his mind but would be identified in the World War II draft. It never happened. Feitig's father believed that "his son may now be somewhere alive suffering from loss of memory. He appealed for aid in locating him." I can still recall seeing Oscar Feitig's picture in his parents' living room whenever I visited them. They never gave up hope that one day he would come home. But he never rang the doorbell; he never came home again, and his room remained empty.

My grandfather kept a Lutheran prayer book in which he wrote various things about family members. On November 14, 1940, he wrote, "Oscar Feitig drowned in Meherin River, South Hill, 9:30 p.m., 1940." He put a newspaper clipping in the prayer book. The clipping has now turned yellow with age. The last words in the prayer book for the day of Oscar Feitig's death are as follows: "O, Lamb of God, I come! I come!"

## Chapter 15

# DISASTER NEAR BYRD AIRPORT

## 1961

On a clear night when I go outdoors to feed the birds, I can see the twinkling stars and airplanes streaking across the night sky. The planes' blinking lights identify an aircraft filled with passengers and crew heading to airports across America and around the world. I never think that the passengers might be in the hands of a crew who are not competent to fly the aircraft. I never imagine anything but perfect decision making in the cockpit, flight attendants who do their jobs and excellent maintenance on the aircraft. After all, flying is the safest means of transportation.

But if I had looked at the Richmond sky on the night of November 8, 1961, I might well have seen a large, four-engine, propeller-driven airplane heading toward Byrd Airport. The aircraft was a Lockheed Constellation, which was shaped like a dolphin and had a triple tail. It was a beautiful plane affectionately called a "Connie." It was leased to Imperial Airlines and was carrying about eighty passengers.

From my backyard, everything would have seemed normal; but if I had been in the cockpit of the airliner with the pilot, copilot and flight engineer, I would have felt stress and seen confusion and frustration. There was chaos in the cockpit. The flight engineer was a student who was being supervised by the official flight engineer, and the plane had two captains, but it was agreed prior to the flight that the more senior captain, James A. Greenlee, would act as the copilot and the less senior captain, Ronald H. Conway, would be the pilot for the flight. This somewhat unusual arrangement would create some command and

The imperial airliner that crashed near Byrd Airport. *Author's collection.*

decision problems in the hours ahead. Questions would arise about who was doing what and who was actually in command. But no one knew that the routine flight of this nonscheduled airliner would soon evolve into panic mode and then into a disaster that would result in the worst airplane crash in Virginia history.

The airplane flying south of Richmond on that night was chartered Imperial Airlines Flight 201/8 flying from Baltimore with seventy-four passengers who had just joined the army and were headed to Fort Jackson, South Carolina, for training. For many of these recruits, this was both their first airplane flight and the first time that they had been away from home. Most of them had been drafted into the army. Reportedly, they were telling jokes as they boarded the plane in Baltimore.

Somewhere near Washington, D.C., the fuel pressure warning lights for engines three and four came on—the number three engine stopped working and the number four engine was not operating properly. The problem was a lack of fuel getting to the two engines. Desperate efforts were made to transfer fuel to restart engine four, but the crew was unable to do this because they did not know the proper procedure to use to transfer fuel. They then tried to restart engine three but were not successful. After they were unable to start the two engines on the right side of the aircraft, they feathered (cut off) the two propellers. Engines one and two were running normally on the left side of the airplane.

Soon, the pilot could see the lights of Richmond, and he decided to land at Byrd Airport. The first contact with the Richmond tower was made at 9:12 p.m. In response to the call to the Richmond tower, the pilot was advised that all runways were available, as was emergency equipment. By this time, the plane was south of Richmond and would use runway number thirty-three.

The situation was critical. Engines three and four still could not be restarted. The passengers were told of the change in plans to land in Richmond, but they were not given instruction about emergency landing procedures since the crew did not anticipate any problems. If such instructions had been given, lives might have been saved. Surely, the passengers must have sensed something was wrong since two engines were not working and the flight plans were changed. Byrd Airport cleared all runways as the plane was getting closer to Richmond. The tower was told the plan was to use runway thirty-three. Then Captain Greenlaw, who was acting as copilot, said, "Let's land on runway two." He lowered the landing gear, but the landing gear wasn't functioning properly. The flight crew then realized that they were too high to land on runway two. The landing gear was lowered manually, but the nose gear would not operate. The pilot asked for full power on engines one and two, and they thought they could make runway thirty-three. The pilot put the airplane in a nose-high altitude at the slowest possible airspeed so the impact would not be too great. Then engine one began to lose power. The plane could not fly on only one engine. The aircraft was doomed.

Conway reported, "The aircraft was slightly to the left of the extended runway centerline on final approach when the airspeed began to decay rapidly." He realized they would not make the runway and pulled back on the control column. His last recollection was of the aircraft stalling into the trees at about ninety-five knots.

Captain Conway said, "I saw the trees coming up. We only clipped the trees. The impact did not seem like anything. But then I realized the airplane was on fire. Everything caught fire immediately. It was bright as daylight outside. The right wing tore into a tree of approximately three feet in circumference, tearing out the tree by its roots." In spite of the lack of power, the landing was level. The plane tore down trees for about one hundred feet and left metal strewn on the ground before it came to rest between Charles City and Portugee Roads, or about half a mile to the left of the final approach path and one mile from the runway in a place that was difficult to reach. The right wing was ripped off, and the rudder was torn from the plane and was about fifty feet from the rest of the aircraft. It was 9:23 p.m.

The crippled plane had ended up "toward the bottom of a gently sloping ravine filled with marshy ground, scrub pine, and undergrowth."

One observer who saw the crippled plane trying to land commented that the plane disappeared behind the trees then "suddenly the horizon lit up. After the pinkish glow died down, a great ball of flames came up." A tower operator stated, "I saw a yellow light off to the left side of the plane. The aircraft then disappeared from view, and about 9:24 p.m., a bright flash was observed."

Two members of the flight crew were able to get out of the plane, but the soldiers, as well as the rest of the flight crew, were trapped in the burning plane. The passengers got out of their seats and tried to get out of the inferno, but they could not open the door and died of carbon monoxide poisoning. They had not been told how to escape. One can only imagine the desperate efforts to open a door that would have permitted a chance to survive. The passengers were trapped in a flaming inferno.

A fireman arrived on the scene and commented that "the woods lit up and I saw two people wandering around." These were the two survivors of the crash. They were Ronald Conway, the twenty-nine-year-old pilot, and the flight engineer, William Poythress, who was thirty years old. The pilot had fallen out of the cockpit, and the flight engineer had managed to jump through the fire. Both survivors knew they could do nothing to save those trapped in the burning fuselage.

The *Richmond News Leader* reported, "The scene was a macabre one with police by the scores, firemen by the dozen, the curious by the hundreds—gathered about the wreckage were generators and spotlights for the fire apparatus." For over four hours, the plane burned in spite of the foam and water that were poured onto it. The only recognizable part of the plane was its triple tail, which was a unique characteristic of the aircraft. Some curious people actually stood on the tail to observe the crash site.

Fire units from Richmond, Henrico and Chesterfield responded to the scene, but they could do nothing. A spokesman for the Civil Air Patrol commented, "There's nothing anybody can do here now but try to contain the fire. There were no survivors to rescue." To reach the fire scene, the equipment had to plow through "mud, water, and gullies." Over one hundred firefighters and other first responders were present in an effort to put out the fire. To provide food, the Red Cross and the Salvation Army arrived on the scene. For traffic control, police from several jurisdictions tried to control the traffic and the crowds. Until the fires were extinguished, army vehicles could only wait until they could reach the aircraft and remove the bodies. Fort Lee soldiers armed with carbines were on site to provide security, as was the FBI.

When the fire was extinguished, the bodies were taken to the Medical College of Virginia for identification. Over one hundred physicians were summoned to help with the bodies. Upon arrival, "bodies were taken to a temporary morgue in McGuire Hall, 77 people died...It was the worst aircraft disaster in Virginia history."

The bodies of the soldiers were taken from MCV to Fort Lee in vans. Fort Lee "soldiers lined the road as the convoy neared the field house. When the procession rolled by, army officers saluted and enlisted men snapped their rifles to present arms. The huge post flag was placed at half-staff where it remained as long as the bodies were at the post."

It was reported that the deaths were by suffocation. Many of the bodies were reportedly found piled up next to the exit door. Most of those who perished were from New Jersey, Maryland and Pennsylvania. The shock to the families was overwhelming. When they found out that the crash was a result of incompetence, their emotions ran out of control. It is one thing to die in combat for your country, but it makes no sense to die because the flight crew was incompetent.

The Civil Aeronautics Board (CAB) determined the probable cause of this accident was the lack of command coordination and decision making, lack of judgment and lack of knowledge of the equipment, resulting in the loss of power in the engines, creating an emergency situation that the crew could not handle. The CAB commented, "It was a tragedy of errors, against a backdrop of confusion, mismanagement and ignorance." It was later revealed that federal law required the government to transport soldiers on the airline that made the lowest bid. After this disaster, the law was changed.

Today, it is difficult to find the place where almost eighty people died a tragic death that was the result of incompetence. Perhaps it is a good thing that nature has reclaimed the place. The recruits never had a chance to serve their country. But when I look up at the star-spangled sky, I still remember them.

# Epilogue
# THE FIRE DANCE

## 2015

I began this book by writing about the disaster at the Sheraton Boston Hotel, where I was recruiting faculty for Virginia Commonwealth University. It seems only appropriate to end it with another personal disaster.

One night, I went into cardiac arrest. While my wife kept shaking me, talking to me and trying to keep me awake, my daughter called 911, and Henrico County Engines 17 and 8, Fire Medic 9 and EMS 1 responded from their stations. With red lights flashing, they came to my house and started doing everything possible to save me, but my heart stopped twice. While all of this was going on, I had a strange dream. I dreamed that I was in a room, tied to the floor, and fire was coming from the floor and the ceiling. Around me were dancing women, and standing over my head was a fireman directing them. I was so angry. I wanted to report them to the county manager. How could people be dancing while I was dying? Two weeks later, I learned that they were not dancing girls but paramedics from Stations 8, 9 and 17. When I met them after I recovered, they did not look a thing like dancing girls. Perhaps the best thing I can write is that, but for the Henrico County Division of Fire and the staff of Henrico Doctor's Hospital, this book would not have been written.

More real than dancing girls were the visits from the two ministers, Alex Evans and Kathryn Lester-Bacon, from my church, Second Presbyterian. Their prayers will always be treasured memories that made a real difference in my recovery. Unlike my experience with the dancing girls, I saw them (the ministers) as angels, and they were very real to me.

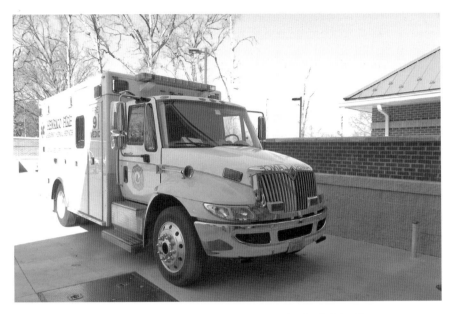

Fire Medic 9 where the fire dance took place. *Photograph by Walter S. Griggs Jr.*

Some of the firefighters from Station 17 whom I mistook for dancing girls. *Photograph by Walter S. Griggs Jr.*

I am still wondering why I survived when the odds were only about 10 percent in my favor.

I also would like to thank fire chief Anthony "Tony" McDowell of the Henrico Division of Fire, who visited me and gave me a fire department patch, which is now in my office next to the words of "Amazing Grace." Together they remind me that God and man saved my life.

Finally, I would thank all those who visited me in the hospital and the students at VCU who sent me cards, letters, flowers and a stuffed moose. I learned that a visit from a friend is far better than watching *General Hospital* on television or even seeing dancing women.

# BIBLIOGRAPHY

## Books

Baker, Meredith Henne. *The Richmond Theater Fire*. Baton Rouge: Louisiana State University Press, 2012.

Barry, John M. *The Great Influenza*. London: Penguin Books, 2004.

Blanton, Wyndham B. *The Making of a Downtown Church*. Richmond, VA: John Knox Press, 1946.

Brown, Alexander Crosby. *The Steamboat Pocahontas, 1893–1939*. Newport News, VA: Mariner's Museum, 1947.

Christian, George L. *The Capitol Disaster: A Chapter of Reconstruction in Virginia*. Richmond, VA: Richmond Press, Inc., 1915.

Christian, W. Asbury. *Richmond: Her Past and Present*. Richmond, VA: L.H. Jenkins, 1912.

Dabney, Virginius. *Richmond: The Story of a City*. Charlottesville: University of Virginia Press, 1990.

Dawson, Henry B. *Battles of the United States by Sea and Land*. New York: Johnson, Fry and Company, 1858.

Fisher, George D. *History and Reminiscences of the Monumental Church*. Richmond, VA: Whittet and Shepperson, 1880.

Furgurson, Ernest B. *Ashes of Glory*. New York: Random House, 1996.

Griggs, Walter S., Jr. *The Collapse of Richmond's Church Hill Tunnel*. Charleston, SC: The History Press, 2011.

Harris, Jay. *Richmond Flood*. Lubbock, TX: C.F. Boone, 1972.

Herbert, Paul N. *The Jefferson Hotel: The History of a Richmond Landmark*. Charleston, SC: The History Press, 2012.

Hoehling, A.A., and Mary Hoehling. *The Day Richmond Died*. New York: A.S. Barnes and Company, Inc., 1981.

Jones, John B. *A Rebel War Clerk's Diary*. New York: A.S. Barnes and Company, Inc., 1961.

Lankford, Nelson. *Richmond Burning*. London: Penguin Books, 2003.

Manarin, Louis H., ed. *Richmond at War*. Chapel Hill: University of North Carolina Press, 1966.

Mordecai, Samuel. *Richmond in By-Gone Days*. Richmond, VA: Dietz Press, Inc., 1946.

Randall, Willard Sterne. *Benedict Arnold: Patriot and Traitor*. New York: Morrow, 1990.

Sanford, James K. *Richmond Her Triumph, Tragedies, and Growth*. Richmond, VA: Metropolitan Richmond Chamber of Commerce, 1975.

Taylor, L.B., Jr. *The Ghosts of Virginia*. Vol. 5. N.p.: Progress Printing Company, 2000.

Thomas, Emory M. *The Confederate State of Richmond*. New York: Harper and Row, 1979.

van Loon, Hendrik Willem. *The Story of Mankind*. New York: Pocket Books, 1921.

von Ewald, Johann. *Diary of the American War*. New Haven, CT: Yale University Press, 1979.

Weddell, Elizabeth Wright. *St. Paul's Church*. Richmond,VA: William Byrd Press, 1931.

# *Newspapers*

*Albany (NY) Argus*, March 26, 1839.
*Alexandria (VA) Gazette*, September 12, 1840; April 28, 1870; May 2, 1904.
*American Journal and General Advertiser* (Providence, RI), January 20, 1781.
*Boston (MA) Herald*, March 31, 1971.
*Boston (MA) Independent Chronicle*, February 1, 1781.
*Burlington (VT) Free Press*, March 29, 1839.
*Chesterfield (VT) Observer*, August 3, 2011.
*Collegian Messenger* (University of Richmond), November 22, 1918.
*Connecticut Journal* (New Haven, CT), February 15, 1781.
*Daily National Intelligencer* (Washington, D.C.), March 25, 1839.
*Free Lance*, May 3, 1904.
*Memphis (TN) Daily Appeal*, May 2, 1870.
*Newark (NJ) Advertiser*, March 26, 1839.
*New Haven (CT) Daily Herald*, vol. 7, issue 79, page 2.
*New Jersey Gazette* (Trenton, NJ), January 24, 1781.
*North American* (Philadelphia, PA), March 27, 1839.
*North Carolina Standard*, April 3, 1839.
*Norwich (CT) Packet*, January 8, 1781.
*Pennsylvania Evening Post* (Philadelphia, PA), January 13, 1781.
*Pennsylvania Journal* (Philadelphia, PA), January 24, 1781.
*Pennsylvania Packet* (Philadelphia, PA), January 19, 1781.
*Rhode Island Republican* (Newport, RI), Vol. 3, March 27, 1839.
*Richmond (VA) Daily Dispatch*, April 1, 1865.
*Richmond (VA) Dispatch*, October 27, 1895.
*Richmond (VA) Enquirer*, March 14, 1863; March 21, 1839; March 23, 1839.
*Richmond (VA) Examiner*, March 14, 1863.

*Richmond (VA) News Leader*, March 13, 1944; February 7, 1962.

*Richmond (VA) Times-Dispatch*, July 30, 1902; July 31, 1903; May 1, 1904; May 3, 1904; May 13, 1904; June 3, 1904; June 24, 1904; June 25, 1904; July 20, 1904; November 8, 1904; November 20, 1904; November 24, 1904; February 2, 1912; September 28, 1918; October 1, 1918; October 3, 1918; October 4, 1918; October 5, 1918; October 6, 1918; October 7, 1918; October 8, 1918; October 9, 1918; October 11, 1918; October 12, 1918; October 13, 1918; October 14, 1918; October 16, 1918; October 17, 1918; October 18, 1918; October 19, 1918; October 20, 1918; October 31, 1918; November 1, 1918; November 3, 1918; November 5, 1918; November 6, 1918; November 10, 1918; November 11, 1918; November 12, 1918; November 20, 1918; December 3, 1918; December 10, 1918; January 4, 1919; January 23, 1919; February 13, 1919; February 15, 1919; March 3, 1919; September 27, 1919; February 1, 1920; March 14, 1921; October 27, 1938; November 16, 1940; November 20, 1940; November 17, 1940; November 18, 1940; November 19, 1940; November 21, 1940; November 22, 1940; November 23, 1940; November 24, 1940; December 4, 1940; December 20, 1940; March 11, 1944; March 12, 1944; March 15, 1944; March 26, 1944; November 28, 1955; January 1, 1960; January 6, 1960; November 11, 1961; November 9, 1962; November 10, 1962; June 16, 1972; June 18, 1972; June 19, 1972; June 21, 1972; June 22, 1972; June 23, 1972; June 24, 1972; June 25, 1972; June 27, 1972; June 29, 1972; June 30, 1972; July 1, 1972; July 2, 1972; November 12, 1977.

*Richmond (VA) Times*, March 30, 1901; March 31, 1901; June 25, 1904; November 20, 1904; March 30, 1911.

*Richmond (VA) Whig* April 4, 1865; April 6, 1865; April 15, 1865.

*Vermont Phoenix*, March 29, 1839.

*Washington, D.C. Evening Star*, April 28, 1870; April 12, 1905.

*Wyandot County (OH) Republican*, May 6, 1870.

## *Miscellaneous Material*

Civil Aeronautics Board Imperial Airline Byrd Field. Richmond, VA, November 8, 1961.

Division of Mineral Resources, publication 85. Richmond, VA.

*Ellyson v. Cahoon*. 19 Grattan 673 (Virgina Reports, 1870).

Rarely Seen Richmond. Virginia Commonwealth University Library, Richmond, VA.

Richmond Clipping File. Richmond Public Library, Richmond, VA.

Virginia Division of Natural Resources, publication 85.

Wilkes, Gerald P. Mining. "History of the Richmond Coalfields of Virginia." Charlottesville, VA: Division of Mineral Resources, 1988.

# *Magazines*

"Letters to Thomas Adams." *Virginia Magazine of History and Biography* 5, no. 3 (January 1898).

Salmon, Emily J. "The Belle of the Nineties." *Virginia Cavalcade* (Summer 1995).

Shackelford, George Green. "Benedict Arnold in Richmond. January 1781." *Virginia Magazine of History and Biography* 60, no. 4 (October 1952).

Weaver, Bettie Woodson. "The Mines of Midlothian." *Virginia Cavalcade* (Winter 1961–62).

# ABOUT THE AUTHOR

**D**r. Walter S. Griggs Jr. is a professor at Virginia Commonwealth University in Richmond, Virginia, where he teaches law. He has also taught history courses in the Honors College. He holds a master's degree from the University of Richmond, a juris doctorate from the University of Richmond School of Law and a doctorate from the College of William and Mary in Virginia. Griggs has written the following books, published by The History Press: *The Collapse of Richmond's Church Hill Tunnel*; *The Hidden History of Richmond*; *World War II Richmond, Virginia*; and *Richmond, Virginia, and the* Titanic. He has also written books on the Civil War, fire departments and moose. He was awarded the Jefferson Davis Medal for his Civil War books and articles. Griggs is married to the former Frances Pitchford, who is, fortunately, a retired English teacher and librarian. She edits and proofs his work. He is also fortunate to have a daughter, Cara, who is a reference archivist for the Library of Virginia. Walter Griggs and his family live in Henrico, Virginia.